Sue Kreitzman frequently appears on BBC1's 'Daytime Live', demonstrating Slim Cuisine dishes to an enthusiastic viewing audience. A native of the USA, she is the author of six American cookery books: *The Nutrition Cookbook*, *Sunday Best*, *Garlic*, *Deli*, *Comfort Food* and *Potatoes*. Sue Kreitzman lives in Cambridgeshire with her husband, nutrition expert Dr Stephen Kreitzman, and her teenage son, Shawm, a dedicated horn student.

Also by Sue Kreitzman
CAMBRIDGE SLIM CUISINE
and published by Corgi Books

SUE KREITZMAN

Cambridge

Slim Cuisine: A Second Helping

CORGI BOOKS

For Annie Coxon

SLIM CUISINE: A SECOND HELPING

A CORGI BOOK   0 552 13578 X

First publication in Great Britain

PRINTING HISTORY
Corgi edition published 1989

Acknowledgement is made to The Token House,
High Street/Peascod Street, Windsor and
O'Connor Brothers, Trinity Yard,
St Leonards Road, Windsor, who kindly loaned
props for the photographs in this book.

Line illustrations by Oriol Bath.
Photographs by Sue Atkinson.

This book is set in 11/12pt Linotron 202 Palatino by
Rowland Phototypesetting Ltd, Bury St Edmunds, Suffolk

Corgi Books are published by Transworld Publishers Ltd,
61–63 Uxbridge Road, Ealing, London W5 5SA, in Australia by
Transworld Publishers (Australia) Pty Ltd, 15–23 Helles
Avenue, Moorebank, NSW 2170, and in New Zealand by Transworld
Publishers (N.Z.) Ltd, Cnr Moselle and Waipareira Avenues,
Henderson, Auckland.

Made and printed in Great Britain by
Mackays of Chatham plc, Chatham, Kent

Captions for Photographs

Photographs between pages 22 and 23:-

What would life be without pudding? Indulge your sweet tooth without widening your waistline: orange jelly in a meringue nest; fudgy chocolate torte; black and white meringue cookies; and cherries in honeyed cream.

A traditional English 'fry'-up breakfast (page 33), minus the grease.

Photographs between pages 54 and 55:-

An elegant picnic (page 33), worthy of Glyndebourne or Henley: gazpacho; stuffed mushrooms; smoked chicken pesto potato salad; and strawberries with raspberry sauce.

Couscous with curried vegetables and spicy lamb meatballs (pages 101 and 82) make a festive party meal.

A luxurious dinner party: chicken liver paté (page 41); meltingly tender veal shanks with wild mushrooms (page 74); polenta with aubergine (page 114), poached pears in honeyed red wine (page 142).

California-style cioppino (page 58) is an exhilarating fish and shellfish soup/stew. Serve it with croutons topped with red pepper-garlic spread.

Photographs between pages 86 and 87:-

Eat Christmas dinner and survive slimly! Slim Cuisine roast turkey; roast potatoes; spicy sprouts; and sausage chestnut stuffing.

Warming hearty soups lighten the gloomiest moods: new-fashioned red pepper-tomato borscht with veal potato balls (page 48); and old-fashioned vegetable soup.

Photographs between pages 118 and 119:-

Italian delights: baked courgettes (page 127); pasta in creamy fennel sauce (page 101); vegetarian lasagne (page 104).

Sinless (yet sensual) Sunday lunch (page 31): pot-roasted leg of lamb; roast potatoes; braised carrots and whipped swedes.

Photographs between pages 150 and 151:-

Sumptuous vegetarian feasts: vegetable chilli with rice (page 103); chilaquiles with tortilla chips, sweet corn and kidney beans (page 99).

Invoke the spirit of Indian cookery without the butterfat: samosa (page 39); Tandoori-style chicken legs (page 91); and spicy potato salad (page 135).

Contents

Acknowledgements

Sandie Perry and Rosemarie Espley, my kitchen assistant and my secretary, make my working life a great pleasure. Besides working hard in the kitchen and at the word processor, they are both ready at all times to drop everything and rush madly around the country, helping me cook, teach and lecture. We have shared many food adventures together, from cooking for foreign royalty to feeding 180 scientists in the dining hall of one of the Cambridge colleges. They are fun to be with, look terrific and I can never thank them enough.

Mary Hardy acts as our housemother, and – as always – helps in many ways. She is an important part of my life in England, and I thank her too.

Thank you also to Sue Atkinson who understands Slim Cuisine very well and photographs it with great sensitivity, to her home economist Elaine Andrews, to my agent David Grossman who has a warm heart and an infectious laugh, to Sally Gaminara, Averil Ashfield, Lizzie Laczynska and Oriol Bath who helped make both *Slim Cuisine*s such handsome volumes, to Dr Ann Coxon, whose support of and enthusiasm for Slim Cuisine is greatly appreciated, to Alan N. Howard, and to Ellee Moules at the *Cambridge Evening News*. And thanks to Robert Parsons for working so hard to make a low-fat cocoa powder available to British chocoholics.

Warm and grateful thanks to the BBC's Mary Clyne and Vicky Kimm who have become valued friends as well as colleagues, and to all the rest of the 'Daytime Live' folks: the secretaries who cheerfully dealt with sacks of requests for Slim Cuisine fact sheets, Judi Spiers (who has refined repartee to a fine art) and Alan Titchmarsh, in addition to all the camera and sound people, the directors, producers and floor managers, *et al.* You all helped to make this past year such *fun*!

Unlimited and loving thanks to my family: to my son Shawm whose surreal conversation never bores me, whose horn-playing always moves me, and whose writing ability has far outstripped that of his parents; and to my husband Steve, who has taught me to think like a scientist, and whose love and support are the mainstays of my life.

Finally, thank you to all the people who took *Slim Cuisine I* to their collective bosoms, who cook the recipes, send me wonderful letters, and have let me know in no uncertain terms that a hedonistic approach to low-fat cookery is just what the world needs.

Preface

'They had lunched, as was their wont, on sugar, starches, oils
and butter-fats. Usually they ate sandwiches of spongy new
white bread greased with butter and mayonnaise . . . thick
wedges of cake lying wetly beneath ice cream and whipped cream
and melted chocolate gritty with nuts . . . patties sweating beads
of inferior oils containing bits of bland meat bogged in pale,
stiffening sauce . . . pastries limber under rigid icing filled with
indeterminate sweet stuff, not yet solid, not yet liquid, like salve
that has been left out in the sun. They chose no other sort of food,
nor did they consider it.'

Dorothy Parker, *The Standard of Living*

The concept of Slim Cuisine is a direct result of my own personal
battle with obesity, and my attempt to achieve, after a 6½ stone
weight loss since 1982, a beautifully balanced state of slim happiness, nutritional well-being and gastronomic satisfaction. Tasteless food, compulsive Calorie counting and grim dietetics are
anathema to me, yet I *never* want to weigh 15-plus stone again, and
I never want to hop on to that bleak and self-defeating see-saw of
gluttony/starvation.

This book, the sequel to *Slim Cuisine*, which was published in
1988, should really be called *Slim Cuisine II, the Fight against Fat
Continues*. Maintaining a large weight loss is a lifetime affair. I feel
those 6½ lost stones of quivering schmaltz haunting me. They
hover, waiting for the first slip, the first heedless slide into the
fat-filled abyss that surrounds every ex-fatty. I have learned how to
shun added dietary fat, yet enjoy good food. I have learned to

ignore the blaring commands of a fat-crazed world, a world dedicated, it sometimes seems, to making ex-fatties fat again. If I, the mother of all food-lovers, can do it, you can too. Stick with me through this sequel. Learn to eat pastries, soufflés, chocolate cream sauce and bread puddings. Learn how to prepare a full-dress Sunday lunch, an epic Christmas dinner, a full English breakfast. Learn to do this while maintaining a radiant and healthy slimness, in fact, learn to *lose* weight with Slim Cuisine, if you need to. And most important, learn how to experience the *therapeutic binge* – specially developed for those who find an occasional bout of over-eating good for the soul. Be happy, be slim, be well-fed – in short, be the master – or mistress – of your own destiny.

Introduction

'The philosophy of this kitchen rests on deep resources of eggs, cream and butter, shinbone marrow, boiled pig skins, and polysaturated pâtés of rich country meat. "Deny yourself nothing" is the motto . . .'

John McPhee, *Brigande De Cuisine*

Join the Revolution

Once upon a time, fat was necessary for survival. Dwelling places were not well heated and clothes and fabrics were not nearly as efficient as they are now at keeping out the cold. Labour-saving devices were unknown. People in every walk of life expended much more energy from day to day, whether they were farmers, labourers, housewives, secretaries . . . Fat-Calorie dense foods were vital for warmth, for work and to make some stored fat for the inevitable lean times ahead. But here we are in the last years of the twentieth century, bombarded with newer and more efficient ways of lightening our workload every day. Tractors and cars have power steering; the manual typewriter gave way to the electric version which in turn fell prey to the word processor. Telephones dial themselves, food processors chop the vegetables, washing machines clean the clothes, and escalators and lifts whisk us upstairs and down. Galloping technology and an ample food supply have drastically decreased our bodies' needs for fat-Calories, yet the culinary arts and sciences have stayed blindly in the past. Recipes still insist on the need to sauté in quantities of butter, stir-fry in oil, lard and bard with animal fat, enrich with

1

cream, sprinkle with high-fat cheese and, in general, pile on the fat in frightening and prodigious quantity. Think of the dollops of clotted cream and whipped cream, the lashings of butter and margarine, the turgid lakes of oil and drippings, the hunks of Cheddar and Brie, the fistfuls of nuts, the greasy mountains of fish and chips and hamburgers and crisps you have consumed in your lifetime. These fat-laden foods doggedly continue to pile on stored fat that you do not need; indeed, that you hate with all your heart and soul. Why cling tenaciously to outmoded and dangerous traditions? If your typewriter and lawn mower are electric, your car is power-steered and your laundry is automatically washed and spun dry, then you must bring the revolution into the kitchen too, or you will be caught in a headlong and inevitable spiral into obesity. Many people have already faced this problem and use drastic dieting to periodically stop the fat binge, and to temporarily reduce the unattractive and unhealthy excess body fat. But crash dieting can't go on forever. Continually alternating such diets with periods of high-fat foods results in a way of life that is both physically and mentally unhealthy.

'The bonds linking us were compulsory starvation, the dreams of food, and the drastic measures required to maintain our diets.'

Gelsey Kirkland, *Dancing on My Grave*

It's time to beat the tradition. Stop depending on fat-based cookery methods. You may save your life. You will certainly hold obesity at bay.

But, alas, tradition is hard to undo. Fat has been the basis of the world's cuisines for countless centuries. In fact, the classic way to identify a particular cuisine is through its flavour principle: a particular fat plus characteristic seasonings. Lard, paprika, marjoram and sour cream immediately identify a dish as Hungarian; olive oil, garlic and herbs place a dish firmly in the Mediterranean; butter, cream and tarragon are indisputably classic French; olive oil, lemon and oregano, Greek; and so on. Thus the fat imparts an identifying flavour to a cuisine, and is inextricably identified with that cuisine. But it does much more; it contributes a huge dose of Calories as well. And at a minimum of 9 Calories per gram, fat has more than twice the Calories of carbohydrate or protein. What's more, evidence shows that dietary fat gets converted into body fat much more quickly and efficiently than carbohydrate and protein. And fat, both saturated and unsaturated, has been implicated in all sorts of diseases in addition to obesity.

2

My purpose in developing Slim Cuisine is finally to beat the system and eliminate the added fat once and for all. All sorts of new techniques and tricks have been substituted for the old fat-based ones. As a result, the food – although extremely low in fat – is quite delicious, and *large portions* will not add to the fat stores. It would be wrong to think it acceptable to add *tiny* bits of fat here and there. Perhaps you think that a mere teaspoon of butter, margarine, or oil used to sauté the onions won't hurt. Avoid that teaspoon of fat like the plague. Don't spread even a sliver of margarine on your bread. And avoid low-fat spreads as well. They are *lower* in fat than butter and margarine, but they are a long way from being no-fat. We are a nation, indeed a world, of fatoholics. The only way to recover from such an addiction is to avoid the noxious substance entirely. An alcoholic does not take a few drops of brandy or whisky each day; so must you not ingest even half a teaspoon of oil a day. Don't keep the stuff in the house or you will find yourself having a drizzle here, a dollop there, and soon your ugly fat stores will be filling up hatefully again.

We *do* have a need for a certain amount of fat in our diets, but the generous variety of meat, fish, poultry, whole grains and vegetables you will be consuming on the Slim Cuisine regime will provide more than enough of the essential fats needed. There is no need for *added* fat.

Slim Cuisine is not a difficult or arduous way of kitchen life. It is no harder than any sort of everyday cookery. Practise its simple precepts, and your cookery will catch up with the rest of your life-style. Remember, this is the late twentieth century, even in the kitchen.

'He is the fat cook not only because of his personal avoirdupois but also because he writes his signature with butter on a dish already heavy with suet and cream.'

John Thorne, *Simple Cooking*

The Slim Cuisine Regime

Use Slim Cuisine as follows to achieve a perfect balance: *slim happiness, nutritional well-being* and *gastronomic satisfaction*.

1   If you love red meat, eat lean meat 3–4 times a week.
2   Egg yolks contain fat, but eggs are a high-protein, vitamin- and mineral-filled food. If you like eggs, eat up to 3 cooked whole eggs a week if you wish. (When counting your whole

egg total, make sure that you include eggs contained in recipes such as Bread Pudding, page 147, as well.) If your blood cholesterol levels are high, however, eat no egg yolks at all. In any case, you may use as many egg *whites* as you wish.

3 Eat a large variety of foods.
4 Eat plenty of whole grains.
5 Eat plenty of potatoes.
6 Eat plenty of fish.
7 Be greedy with vegetables. Eat all you want, cooked any way you want them, as long as the cooking techniques are Slim Cuisine ones. This collection contains many sumptuous all-vegetable recipes (pages 95–120). Indulge frequently and lavishly, especially those marked ♡ (Very Low Fat, see page 11) and ✿ (Therapeutic Binge, see page 11). Raw vegetables make great snacks, especially when dunked in Slim Cuisine spreads and dips. Remember two things about raw vegetables, however.

(a) A little bit of cooking breaks down some of the cell walls in vegetable matter and actually makes some vegetables *more* nutritious, so don't depend on raw vegetables only.

(b) Raw carrot sticks and red and yellow pepper strips are sweet, crisp and juicy – they make extremely satisfying snacks. What's more, they are rich in beta-carotene (your body uses beta-carotene to make vitamin A, one of the fat-soluble vitamins), so it's a good idea for people on fat-free regimes to munch away on these particular vegetables. (Spinach, peas, broccoli, tomatoes, sprouts and apricots are also rich sources of beta-carotene – indulge freely.) And to make them even more attractive, many scientists feel that beta-carotene is a protector against some types of cancer. One word of advice: if the palms of your hands turn a startling orange, or you develop orange splotches on your skin, you may be indulging a little too freely. Large doses of beta-carotene can produce such skin changes. It is not dangerous, but if you want it to fade to your normal colour, cut down on the raw vegetable snacks.

8 Use salt, sugar and artificial sweeteners sparingly. They are seasonings, meant to enhance – not to overpower. They will not harm you in small quantities, but don't get carried away.

9 Alcohol contains 7 empty Calories per gram. I know this is not everyone's happiest news, but if you want to stay slim and healthy, you have a better chance of doing so *without* alcohol. And, if you want to lose weight, you *must* do without it. Use it as a cooking ingredient (heat dissipates the alcohol and thus the alcohol Calories), but stop there.

10 Cut out *all* added fats and high-fat foods: butter, whole or *part*-skimmed milk products, high-fat cheeses, margarine, vegetable oils, drippings, lard, suet, chicken fat, low-fat spreads, hydrogenated shortenings, mayonnaise, salad dressings, nuts, high-fat meats, poultry skin, high-fat baked goods and prepared foods. Use stock as a sauté medium to replace fat (see the Slim Cuisine review section, page 13, and individual recipes).

'Everywhere you turn, food awaits you in huge wondrous quantities. Giant neon burgers dance in circles above your head. A chocolate chip cookie calls your name.'

David Hoffman, *The Joy of Pigging Out*

The Food Day

The food happenings of the day are not confined to mealtimes. Snacking, in-between munching and 'picking' all play an important role in a food-lover's passage through life. Whether that life is an unhealthy one of miserable obesity or one of robust and well-nourished slimness is up to you. You *must* be the master of your own destiny. It seems as if the world is out to make you fat; indeed, it sometimes seems that the world is out to kill you. The media – television, radio, billboards, newspaper and magazine ads – blare loud and persuasive messages. The pictures, sounds and smells of fatty, sugary, salty, ridiculously calorific foods are *everywhere*. The food and drink itself – sugar-coated, salt-sprinkled and dripping mega-fat – is everywhere, too; at eye level and brilliantly packaged in the supermarket, sending forth seductive vapours from fast-food and fish-and-chip emporia, patiently waiting in fizzy anticipation inside soft-drink machines. Because it is there, because you are being inundated with commands to drown yourself mindlessly in it, does not mean that you have to comply.

It can be difficult. I remember standing in the snackbar of a British Rail station, ravenous and exhausted. I was desperate for something to tide me through the long journey home, but there was *nothing* that looked remotely edible by my fat-shunning standards. The girl behind the counter reacted with astonishment when I asked for a sandwich without butter or mayonnaise. 'Madame,' she said, her voice dripping with contempt, 'We can't bother to make things that people *like*, you know.' All through the long train ride I comforted myself with visions of the huge bowlful of mashed potatoes, garnished with all sorts of beguiling things, that I would have as soon as I reached home.

The advantage of the Slim Cuisine regime is that after a few months, high-fat, over-sugared foods lose their charm, indeed they become downright disgusting. Resisting them becomes a pleasure rather than a chore, and mastering your own destiny becomes easy. The media's siren songs become grotesque to your ears, and the foods that you crave are those waiting at home in your fridge, freezer and pantry.

'Off and on the sign went. It was a distant neon arrow pointing down through the night to JACK'S GOLDEN DOME TURNPIKE DINER. EAT . . . EAT . . . EAT . . . EAT . . . it endlessly intoned . . . EAT . . . EAT . . . EAT . . . And so we did.'

Jean Shepherd, *A Fistful of Fig Newtons*

Snack Advice

When the world of sweet bars, confectionery, crisps, and so on, is shut to you, what do you do about between-meal nibbles and treats? Here are some suggestions. They all contribute to the day's overall nutrition and provide fun eating as well.

1 **Raw Vegetables** ❀ ♡ (see page 4) with quark or Slim Cuisine dips. They are crisp (a good snack should crunch), colourful, and many are *sweet*, and so are very satisfying to a sweet tooth.
2 **Fresh Fruit** ♡ . I swoon over greengrocers' displays: tart, snappy apples; green, purple, or red grapes; oranges, blood and otherwise; mangoes; pears; bananas; pineapples; cherries and berries in season; lychees. Why would anyone want to settle for a horrible packaged piece of flabby pastry or an artificially flavoured sweet bar coated with inferior, vegetable-fat injected chocolate, when such a panoply of juicy delight is available at any supermarket? Keep your fridge well stocked, and carry a good supply with you, or learn to stop in the supermarket's fresh produce section when the snack attack hits. Many markets now carry vegetables (and sometimes fruits) all peeled, sliced and ready to eat. This fills my heart with joy and thankfulness.

'Sometimes there would be tangerines, and he would peel off the pock marked orange skin for her and the spongy white threads that laced over the fruit. She would eat the sections one by one, the juice spurting sweet and sharp into her mouth.'

Sylvia Plath, *Among the Bumblebees*

3 **Dried Fruits.** Dried fruits are very concentrated in sweetness and flavour. They make a power-packed snack, because they are low in fat, yet rich in vitamins, minerals and fibre. But be warned. Because they are so concentrated, so delicious, so easy to eat, they can pile on the sugar Calories at top speed. One pound (480 grams) of dried apricots weighs in at approximately 1,179 Calories. That's only about 14 Calories per apricot, but you'd be surprised at how quickly a pound disappears down a snack-loving gullet – especially during relaxed circumstances; watching the telly, reading a good book, and so on. If you are going to snack mindlessly, turn to raw vegetables, tortilla chips and popcorn. If you feel willing to exercise a certain amount of discretion, enjoy dried fruits in sensible amounts. Use them in puddings as well, but don't feel that you can polish off the whole recipe all by yourself. Share it, or hide the leftovers for another day.

4 **Popcorn** ♡ . Make your own in the microwave with *no* fat or oil. A full pint (600 ml) of popcorn contains only 66 Calories, and practically no fat at all. A pint (600 ml) or so of popcorn and a good movie on the video make a very cosy combination.

5 **Tortilla Chips** ♡ (page 97). Make these every once in a while in huge batches, and store them in airtight tins. Eat them plain, or with Mock Guacamole (page 44) or Red Pepper and Garlic Spread (page 45).

6 **Ice Cream** ♡ (page 158). Whip up a batch of Slim Cuisine Instant Ice Cream any time you get the urge. It takes minutes to make and contributes plenty of good things (calcium, protein, vitamins and minerals) to your daily nutrition. And what it does for your daily well-being is immeasurable.

7 **Breakfast Cereals** ♡ . These are the unsung heroes of the snack world. Read the labels and buy those that have no added sugar, salt, or fat. If a brand is fortified with vitamins and minerals, so much the better. Cereals are an excellent source of fibre, and those made with wholemeal grains are a good source of vitamin E, one of the fat-soluble vitamins. When you douse these cereals in milk they turn into a soggy mess, but eaten out of the hand they are crispy and delicious. Perfect snack food, especially for children, who need all the fat-free and sugar-free nutrition they can get. And small shredded wheat, dabbled in Slim Cuisine Chocolate Cream Sauce (page 154), make a very classy sweet bar substitute.

'It was Scott Fitzgerald who ordered shredded wheat at Voisin's.'

Mrs E.C.N., in a letter

8   **Bread** ♡ . I get so irked when people turn away from bread because they are trying watch their weight. Don't be guilty of such nonsense. Snack on bread when you want something delicious, filling and satisfying – don't think of shunning such excellent food. Learn to be a connoisseur; try a variety from different bakeries so that you can see what diversity of choice there is. My favourite breads have a crust that is tough and chewy, or so crisp that it showers the table with a storm of shards as you eat it. I like a fairly dense crumb, too, with a high percentage of whole grain and rye flours. A good slice of bread needs no greasing with butter and margarine; the very thought makes my tastebuds cringe. But if you want something voluptuously creamy on a slice of bread, try a good 'schmeer' (forgive the New Yorkese) of quark, the perfect no-fat spread. Learn to read labels and to quiz the baker. Don't buy breads that have fat or an excess of sugar in their formulation.

'Butter was not rolled into marbles during the 1870s.
Well, we should say not!
It was lifted in half-pound gobs and those who smeared it never felt
    improvident.'

George Ade, *Fables in Slang*

How To Use This Book

'You have fed me wretched food, vegetables boiled to extinction, fistfuls of white sugar, slabs of fat, mucousy casseroles made with gobs of cream of mushroom, until it's amazing that my heart still beats.'

Garrison Keillor, *Lake Wobegon Days*

Kitchen Sense

There is an art to following a recipe and everyone – novice or old kitchen hand – should practise that art if they want to avoid chaos, wasted time and culinary disaster. The rules are simple.

1   First, read the recipe through completely.
2   Then have all the ingredients chopped, sliced, diced, poured, measured, and so on. Set the prepared ingredients out on your work surface.
3   Also set out on your work area any equipment needed. Heed the directions in the recipe. If it calls for a frying pan and a wooden spoon, don't assume that you can get good results by substituting a saucepan and a stainless steel fork. A ☐ or ⑤ indicate the need for a microwave or food processor in a particular recipe. The recipes are well thought out and carefully worded. Don't sabotage them.

Only when these three steps have been carried out should you begin the actual cooking.

Measurement Note

All ingredients are given in imperial and in metric measurements. Use one or the other, but do not mix measurements in any one recipe.

A Note on Technique and Planning

For those who work full time and then come home to cook, weekday meals *must* be quick. It is a terrible shame, though, to succumb to the lure of high-fat packaged and frozen foods because of limited time. And it is even more of a shame to fall back on old familiar techniques – sautéing in butter, margarine, or oil, deep frying, and so on – because you are afraid that the new techniques of Slim Cuisine might be difficult and time-consuming. If you want to stay slim, well-nourished and comforted, make a commitment to a personal kitchen revolution, even if you don't have unlimited kitchen time.

Changing over to Slim Cuisine means learning some new techniques and habits. It takes no longer to do Slim Cuisine than any other kind of cookery, especially if you plan ahead. Here are some planning tips to make life easier and cooking a joy.

1   The Slim Cuisine method of sautéing in stock is easy; don't let it make you nervous. Because it is new, it may seem daunting or difficult as you read each recipe, but once you have actually tried it, you will see how quick and simple it is.
2   Use your freezer to store home-made stocks in small portions, and batches of sautéed onions and mushrooms. And why not, on leisurely days or evenings, make large batches of your favourite recipes. Freeze in small portions. What luxury to just pop a container in the microwave at the end of a hard day. Instant comfort!
3   Home-made stocks are marvellous but time-consuming. If you just don't want to put in the effort, don't worry. Search your local wholefood, health, or speciality food store for good vegetable stock powder or paste, such as Friggs Vegetale (a powder) or Healthrite vegetable stock paste. Although many stock cubes and powders have a characteristic harsh, artificial taste, and contain far too much fat and salt, these two products are excellent. If your local small store does not carry them, ask that they be ordered. Friggs Vegetale is labelled as a low-Calorie vegetable *drink* but – trust me – it makes an excellent vegetable stock for sauté purposes, and it contains no fat. It is not necessary to reconstitute the powder first. Simply combine

whatever you want to sauté with the amount of water given in the recipe, sprinkle in a bit of the powder, and proceed.

4   Always have quark and fromage frais in the fridge, so that you can make gorgeous spreads and salad dressings when you get the urge. Also have on hand at all times: buttermilk, very low fat yoghurt, skimmed milk, medium-fat Mozzarella cheese and Parmesan cheese.

Symbols Used in This Book

Several symbols appear regularly throughout the book, marking various recipes as useful in a particular way. Here is a guide to symbol interpretation.

1   ♡ (Heart Symbol). These are *very* low fat recipes, and very low sugar as well. If you wish to *lose* weight, yet stay well-nourished, confine yourself to these recipes.

2   ✿ (Teddy Bear Symbol). Everyone needs an occasional *therapeutic binge* – an opportunity to eat all they want of something delicious without fear of dire consequences (galloping fat, burgeoning flab, high blood pressure, clogged arteries . . .). If a recipe is marked with a teddy bear, it is suitable for therapeutic bingeing; eat *all you want* of that particular dish. If at the end of your 'binge' your waistband feels too tight and you appear to have developed a definite paunch, fear not. That full feeling and pot belly will disappear in a few hours – in the morning you will feel as slim as ever. Do plan to have therapeutic binges every once in a while. They fill you up beautifully with the best vegetables – very important to your vitamin, mineral and fibre levels – and they give you a marvellous sense of gastronomic freedom.

'The reason diet books don't work for me is that they use terminology I don't begin to understand. "Eat one portion of chicken" they say. As far as I'm concerned, a portion of chicken is a chicken. A portion of beef is a cow. A portion of ice cream is whatever container it happens to come in.'

Peter Feibleman, *Lear's Magazine*

3   ⊕ (Clock symbol). A clock indicates a fast recipe, perfect for those days when you come home late, there is nothing prepared in the freezer, and you want something wonderful to eat. Some of the ⊕ recipes are elegant enough for guests. Some are homely, family-type recipes.

11

4   ❅ (Snowflake symbol). Snowflaked recipes are suitable for freezing. Directions for thawing and reheating (with the microwave and by conventional methods) will be contained in the body of the recipe.

5   ☐ (Microwave symbol). Many recipes in this book call for a microwave oven. Some recipes are followed by microwave adaptations. Such recipes and footnotes are marked with ☐ .

6   ⑤ (Food processor symbol). This symbol indicates a recipe that calls for the use of a food processor.

A Note on Calorie and Fat Counts

In *Slim Cuisine I*, all recipes were meticulously labelled for fat and Calorie values. I have decided *not* to do the same in this book. Nutrition tables used to compute such values give numbers that are only approximate. Nutrient levels in food change with the time of the year, the geographical origin of the food and many other factors. Besides, Calorie counting is boring and self-defeating. When you worry too much about such things, you ruin your eating pleasure, and you may find yourself cutting down too much out of fear of Calories. Because Slim Cuisine cuts out so much fat, the Calorie levels in my recipes are very low in general; in fact, you will save even more Calories than standardized charts would have you think. For a long time it was believed that fat weighed in at 9 Calories per gram. Recent reports from a major research facility in the US suggest that fat may actually be 11 Calories per gram. (Compare that to 4 Calories per gram for carbohydrate and protein!)

It is important to eat lavishly to keep your nutrients and morale high. Use Slim Cuisine techniques religiously, do not succumb to wicked outside temptations, use your common sense, and there will be no need to compute every Calorie. And don't hop on and off the scales every hour, or even every day. There is no need to be obsessive. Check your weight every week or two. If you establish good, steady Slim Cuisine habits, nature will take its course and your weight will be stable. And if you stick to the ♡ recipes for a while, you will *lose* weight in a very well fed manner.

'I am the ringleader of the faction that says, yes, we must diet. We must go to bed hungry and fit back into our clothes and never give in to inertia and complacence.

'So I dieted all summer and in three months I had gained three pounds. Needless to say I do not think this is funny. I think it is very cruel and unfair.'

Ellen Gilchrist, *Falling through Space*

Slim Cuisine: A Review

'All that oil? What is this, oil soup?' Picket . . . picked the book up and took a look at the cover, on which was a picture of a startlingly fat man with a pudding face, grinning out across an appalling lot of sausages. "You're cooking out of this man's book?"'

James P. Blaylock, *The Last Coin*

Stock

Good stock is one of the most important components of Slim Cuisine. It does much to make up for the lack of cooking fats and oils. Stock acts as a superb sautéing medium, and contributes flavour and body. Recipes follow for several basic stocks. If you can fit their making into your kitchen rhythm, your cookery will have a wonderful dimension of depth and vibrancy. (See page 15 for shortcuts, if you don't have time to brew home-made stock.)

♡ 🧸 ❄ BASIC CHICKEN STOCK

Makes approximately 4 pts/2400 ml

This is an improved chicken stock; easier, less expensive and fuller bodied than the one in *Slim Cuisine I*. Order chicken wings from your butcher. They are very inexpensive and make a wonderfully full-bodied stock. It is so rich that it jells when chilled. In my kitchen, my assistant Sandie Perry and I get double our money's worth out of chicken wings by using them twice. After we've drained the solids from a batch of stock, we pick out the wings, combine them with fresh vegetables and do the whole thing over again. As far as I'm concerned, chicken stock is the best sautéing medium there is. Make it regularly in large batches, and freeze it in small batches. Thaw (in the microwave, if you have one) when needed.

2½–3½ lb/1¼–1½ kg chicken wings, plus backs, necks and carcasses if you have them	2 carrots
	1 small onion
	A few garlic cloves, unpeeled
3 celery stalks	Several sprigs of parsley
2 parsnips	Salt

1   Wash the chicken pieces well. Scrub the celery, parsnips and carrots, leaving the carrots and parsnips unpeeled. Peel the onion. Cut the celery, carrots, parsnips and onion into chunks.

2   Boil the chicken parts in 6½ pts/3900 ml of water. After 10 minutes, skim all foam and scum from the top. Add the garlic and vegetables. Reduce the heat so that the liquid stays at a steady simmer. Simmer, partially covered, for 2½–3 hours. Cool.

3   Carefully strain the stock through a fine sieve or strainer. Press down on the solids to extract all their goodness. Pour the stock into clean jars, cover tightly and refrigerate overnight.

4   By the next day the fat will have risen to the top of each jar of stock and solidified. Meticulously scrape away every speck of fat and discard it. Pour the de-fatted stock into freezer containers, label with the date and store in the freezer until needed.

♡ 🧸 ⊕ ❄   **FISH STOCK**

Makes 4 pts/2400 ml

You can usually pick up fish scraps free from your fishmonger. Fish stock is a snap to prepare; it needs to simmer for 30 minutes only. Use it for any of the fish dishes in this collection.

4 lb/1.8 kg fish bones and heads (use lean white fish only; halibut, cod, sole, etc.)	3 stalks celery, coarsely chopped
	½ pt/300 ml dry white wine
	4 pts/2400 ml water
2 large onions, coarsely chopped	Several sprigs parsley
4 carrots, peeled and coarsely chopped	A few peppercorns
	½ bay leaf

1   Rinse fish bones and heads well under cold running water.
2   Combine the chopped vegetables, 2 fl oz/60 ml of wine and ½ pt/300 ml water in a non-reactive pot. Cover and bring to the boil. Boil for 5 minutes. Uncover, lower the heat a bit and simmer until the vegetables are almost tender but not browning, and the liquid is almost gone.
3   Add fish bones and heads and all remaining ingredients. Bring to the boil, reduce heat and simmer, partially covered, for 20–30 minutes. Strain, discard solids, cool and then refrigerate, or freeze in small portions.

♡ ❀ ⊕ ❄ COURT BOULLION

Makes 1½ pts/900 ml

Court boullion is often used for poaching fish and shellfish. Because it takes only 10 minutes to prepare, and has a nice depth of flavour despite that short time, it makes a dandy stock substitute when you have nothing else at hand.

1 large onion, peeled and coarsely diced	1 bay leaf
	2–3 sprigs parsley
1 large carrot, scraped and coarsely diced	1 inch/2.5 cm piece lemon zest
	½ pint/300 ml dry white wine
1 large celery stalk, coarsely diced	2 pts/1200 ml water

1   In a large non-reactive saucepan combine all ingredients except water. Bring to the boil for 2 minutes. Add water. Cover and boil for 10 minutes. Drain. Discard solids.

♡ ❀ ⊕ DESPERATION STOCK

When all else has failed – you are out of home-made stuff, there is no more vegetable stock powder left in the larder, you are tired and hungry and you want to be ready to sauté right *now* – put onions in a heavy non-reactive frying pan with a combination of half water and half dry white wine or dry white vermouth. Sauté as directed (see page 23 for individual recipes).

Sauces

♡ 🧸 🕐 ❄ **TOMATO SAUCE**

Makes 1½ pts/900 ml

Italian tinned tomatoes are an excellent store cupboard item; you should never be without them. Use them to make this basic tomato sauce, useful in so many ways. Tinned tomatoes are almost too good; it is so easy to use them to make a quick, thick, rich no-fat sauce, that you may find yourself reaching for them every evening, when time has been short. Remember, variety is important, for nutrition *and* to avoid boredom.

---

3 shallots, finely chopped
2 cloves garlic, peeled and crushed
Pinch cayenne pepper
6 fl oz/180 ml stock
6 fl oz/180 ml dry red wine, white wine, or vermouth
1 tablespoon chopped fresh parsley
1 tablespoon each chopped fresh basil, thyme and oregano or

¼ teaspoon each dried basil, thyme and oregano
3 tins (14 oz/400 g each) chopped tomatoes
Small piece Parmesan cheese rind
Salt and freshly ground pepper to taste
2 tablespoons tomato paste

---

1 Combine shallots, garlic, cayenne, stock, wine and herbs in a heavy frying pan. Bring to the boil. Reduce heat and simmer briskly until almost all the liquid has been evaporated. Season to taste.

2 Stir in the tomatoes, Parmesan rind, salt and pepper. Simmer, partially covered, for 15 minutes. Stir in the tomato paste and simmer for 5 minutes more. Taste and adjust seasoning. Discard the Parmesan rind. If you want a smooth sauce, purée the mixture in the liquidizer, then rub it through a sieve. If you like your tomato sauce chunky, leave it as it is. Freeze tomato sauce in small portions and thaw when needed.

'The Colonel did the cooking, and tomatoes kept creeping into everything, which gave him delusions of persecution.'

Dorothy Parker, *Mrs Hofstedder on Josephine St.*

PESTO

Makes 12 fl oz/360 ml

One of the most successful and popular Slim Cuisine adaptations of a high-fat classic. Thank goodness that fresh basil is available all year round in the large supermarkets. Life without regular infusions of this brilliant and pungent sauce/spread would be very dull indeed.

Note: Nuts are a high-fat food, and so are not allowed as a snack in the Slim Cuisine regime, but they may be used occasionally as an ingredient (as pine nuts are used here), in very small quantities.

¾ pt/450 ml torn basil leaves	*½ lb/240 g quark*
½ pt/300 ml roughly chopped parsley	*Purée from 2 heads of Baked Garlic (see below)*
5 tablespoons freshly grated Parmesan cheese	*Salt and freshly ground pepper to taste*
1 oz/30 g pine nuts	

---

1   Combine all ingredients in the container of a food processor.
2   Process to a thick paste. Scrape into a bowl and refrigerate. If your quark is very fresh to begin with, the sauce will keep for a week.

Glorious Garlic

I am trying to bring about a garlic revolution in the UK. Fresh, firm, large heads of garlic (never pathetic old withered and sprouting ones) can be baked in the oven so that the meat of each garlic clove turns soft, buttery and *mild*. The garlic purée that results from such baking is one of the most valuable of Slim Cuisine ingredients. It provides mellowness and gorgeous mild flavour, and increases perceived richness in sauces, stews and soups.

   ## BAKED GARLIC

Whole heads of garlic

---

1   Preheat oven to 375° F, 190° C, Gas Mark 4.
2   Remove the papery outer covering of the whole garlic heads, but do not separate the cloves or peel them. Place each whole

head of garlic on a square of foil (shiny side of the foil in). Fold up the foil and crimp so that the head is completely wrapped.

3   Bake in the preheated oven for approximately 1 hour 15 minutes (depending upon size of garlic bulb).

4   Remove from the oven, unwrap and cool for at least 5 minutes. Gently separate the cloves and squeeze each one over a fine-meshed sieve so that the softened garlic pops into the sieve.

5   With a wooden spatula or spoon rub the garlic through the sieve into a small container or bowl. (If you are in a hurry, forget the sieve. Simply squeeze the garlic into the bowl.) Cover tightly with plastic wrap and refrigerate until the purée is needed.

♡ 🧸 🕐 ⌗ MICROWAVE VERSION OF BAKED GARLIC

If you try to put a whole head of garlic into the microwave to bake, you will end up with something quite horrid. The cloves become tough and the taste becomes acrid and revolting. There *is* a way, however, to achieve a melting, mellow and sweetly delicious garlic purée in the microwave. Be *very careful* when you remove the cling film. Follow the directions meticulously, or you may get scalded by the steam.

1   Remove the papery outer covering from 2–3 large, firm heads of garlic, but do not peel them. Separate the cloves. Scatter them, in one layer, in an 8 inch/20 cm square, 1–2 inch/2.5–5 cm deep glass baking dish. Pour in water to a depth of a little more than ½ inch/1.25 cm. Cover *tightly* with microwave cling film.

2   Microwave on high for 10 minutes. Carefully remove from the oven (do not remove or loosen cling film) and let stand for 10 minutes.

3   With tongs peel away a corner of the cling film on the side *away from you*, to allow steam to escape. Be very careful: the steam is hot, and you don't want to get burned. With the tongs, remove the cling film.

4   When the garlic is cool enough to handle, remove the skins (they will slip right off). Drain the garlic and place in a bowl. Mash with a fork or a wooden pestle. If desired, push through a sieve to make a very fine purée.

Glorious Garlic

It's no secret that I love garlic, particularly in quantity. While some people add a clove or two to a sauce, wondering nervously all the while if they are erring on the side of excess, I throw the cloves in by the double handful. In my view, garlic is much more than a seasoning to be used with discretion. The glorious bulb is a vegetable, meant to be used in exhilarating quantity. The fascinating thing about garlic is that the whole cloves, cooked in quantity, gently and slowly, become soft, buttery, mild and sweet – so unlike garlic's usual sharp pungency. Such gentle cooking also renders garlic much more digestible.

The really exciting news is that garlic (like onion), consumed in quantity, is now recognized as a significant health food. Research from both the US National Cancer Institute and the Chinese Institute for Cancer Research suggests that high consumption of garlic and onions may lessen susceptibility to stomach cancer. And many researchers also believe that high consumption of glorious garlic may help bring down high blood pressure and blood cholesterol levels. So if you needed the perfect excuse to have an unbridled allium wallow, you've got it now!

Garlic Breath and Onion Tears

I'm always amazed at the variations in the personal chemistry of people. Some individuals can chop, slice, dice and purée garlic and onions with abandon and never breathe a hint of it or shed the smallest tear. Others merely touch a clove or a bulb of the pungent vegetables and immediately weep buckets while they light up the vicinity with an incandescent allium glow. For those who are sensitive to the volatile chemicals in both onions and garlic, here are a few helpful hints.

1   **Garlic on the Hands.** For some, soap and water work fine. If not, try rubbing your hands with lemon juice or a little salt. If your hands still reek, here is the ultimate foolproof method. It sounds strange, but it really works:

After handling garlic, rub your fingers thoroughly with the bowl of a stainless steel spoon (it *must* be stainless steel), under cold running water, then wash your hands with soap. The metal neutralizes the garlic, and the lingering odour will be gone.

2   **Onion Tears.** There are many folk remedies offered to cure onion tears: chill the onions, freeze them, peel them under

cold running water, peel them with a wooden match clenched between your teeth, handle them near an open window, an extractor fan, an open flame. If you are prone to onion tears and you try one of these methods, you will exclaim 'This method (sob, sniff) does not work!' Wear swimming goggles or a gas mask. It's the only way.

3   **Garlic Breath.** Alas, there are no easy remedies for this. Breath mints and mouth washes and all the folk remedies (parsley, a raw coffee bean, anise seeds) sweeten the mouth, but the problem is not in the mouth; it is in the lungs and in the very pores of the skin. My favourite old remedy is the one that suggests eating vast quantities of garlic every day for a week. Garlic breath, claims Ford Maddox Ford in a famous excerpt from *Provence*, 'attends only those timorous creatures who have not the courage as it were to wallow in that vegetable'. Wrong. If you wallow in garlic you will smell of it.
There is only a partial solution to the problem.
(a) If the garlic is baked, or otherwise gently cooked in a way that makes it mellow, the subsequent odour will be mellow.
(b) See that your family, friends and associates eat as much garlic as (or more than) you do. Then they will all have that allium glow, but no one will notice it. Just remember this: it's chic to reek.

'Now there is no good cooking except with garlic . . .'

Ludwig Bemelmans, *Father Dear Father*

Chillies: Handle with Care

Several Slim Cuisine recipes call for a fresh chilli or two. To those who are sensitive to the volatile oils, preparing chillies can be a painful and even dangerous exercise. You *must* wear rubber gloves while handling chillies; it is the only safe protection. *Never* touch your eyes or any other sensitive area (men, for instance, should not attempt to go to the loo) until the gloves are safely stripped off and stowed away, and your hands are thoroughly washed. Should your eyes or other mucous membranes become burnt or irritated, flush at once with cold water. And if you burn your mouth with a bite of chilli-ridden curry or other too-spicy food, don't attempt to quench the burn with floods of cold drink. Cold drinks exacerbate the problem. Try a bite of bread or banana or a spoonful of honey.

Chilli Powder, Cayenne Pepper, Etc.

Recipes calling for chilli powder have been tested with Schwartz chilli powder. Use mild, hot, or a combination, according to your taste and discretion. Feel free to cut down on the amounts called for, or even to cut them out, if you do not possess an asbestos palate.

'One bite, and your tongue dials the fire department.'

N. Steinberg and D. Palumbo, *My Favourite Year*

Aubergine Purée

Aubergine purée discreetly stretches meat. Used in hamburgers, sausages, and mince sauces such as Bolognese sauce, it allows you to use less meat without affecting the taste. *Lean* meat can be very dry and 'bitty' – aubergine restores moistness and smoothness.

 ## BAKED AUBERGINE

Whole aubergines

1. Preheat oven to 400° F, 200° C, Gas Mark 7.
2. Pierce the aubergines in several places with a fork or thin skewer. Bake directly on the oven rack for 30–40 minutes, until soft and collapsed. Cool.
3. Cut away the stem, strip off and discard the skins, and chop finely or mash. (If the clumps of seeds are large and tough they may be discarded.)

MICROWAVE VERSION OF BAKED AUBERGINE

Aubergines must be pierced before they are microwaved, or they may explode. To make aubergine purée to use as a filler that provides moistness in meatballs, hamburgers and sausages, they must be steamed, in ½ inch/1.25 cm of water. Again, be very careful not to scald yourself with the steam. To roast the aubergine in the microwave so that it can be sliced into deeply flavoured, good-textured pieces, suitable for casseroles, see page 114.

1   Place 1 aubergine (½ lb/240 g) in a 8 inch/20 cm square, 1–2 inch/2.5–5 cm deep glass baking dish. Pour in ½ inch/1.25 cm water. Cover tightly with microwave cling film. Microwave on high for 6 minutes. Remove from the oven. Do not uncover. Let rest for 5 minutes.
2   With tongs, very carefully peel away one corner of the cling film on the side away from you to allow steam to escape. It is very hot, so use caution, you do not want to scald your hand or face. With the tongs, remove cling film. When the aubergine is cool enough to handle, strip off the skin with a dull knife. Chop the pulp very finely with a chef's knife.

♡ 🧸 🕑 ❄ Sautéed Mushrooms

The Slim Cuisine fat-free mushroom sauté method results in mushrooms that are so vivid with mushroom flavour, they are an almost supernatural fungi essence. The more types of mushroom you use, the better. See page 118 for a mushroom ragoût that adds dried mushrooms as well, for even more mushroominess.

Leave button mushrooms whole if desired – larger mushrooms may be sliced or cut into quarters or eighths. It is fun to use a variety of fresh mushrooms: field, chestnut, shiitake, oyster, etc. Sauté them in the 'Holy Trinity' of mushroom cookery: stock, dry sherry and soy sauce (or teriyaki sauce). Sometimes I add a splash of balsamic vinegar as well. Spread the mushrooms out in a heavy-bottomed (enamelled cast iron is best) pan, and pour in 2–3 fl oz/60–90 ml of each liquid, and a splash of balsamic vinegar, if you are using it. Cook over high heat, stirring. The mushrooms will release a great deal of liquid. Keep on cooking, stirring occasionally, until the liquid has been absorbed, and the mushrooms are 'frying' in their own juices. *Never* let the mushrooms scorch, burn, or stick to the pan. Season with freshly ground pepper. These mushrooms may be prepared ahead of time and stored in the fridge. They also freeze well. They may be cooked in a non-stick frying pan, or a heavy enamelled cast iron one.

'After an hour or so in the woods, looking for mushrooms, Dad said "Well, we can always go to the store and buy some real ones."'

John Cage, *A Year from Monday*

Onions

'Fried' onions are the pride and joy of Slim Cuisine, and a good illustration of the no-fat stock sauté method. Who would guess that

this mass of meltingly tender, syrupy, amber brown, tantalizingly odorous 'fried' onions is *diet* food!? My son eats these regularly, heaped on to a Slim Cuisine hamburger (see *Slim Cuisine I*), enclosed in a bap spread with ketchup on its lower half and New York Deli Mustard (page 138) on its upper. I eat the same thing, without the hamburger. Fried onion sandwiches! What bliss. If you wish, the onions may be chopped or sliced, instead of being cut into wedges. Please note that the onions should be cooked in an enamelled cast iron frying pan, *not* a non-stick one.

♡ 🐻 ⊕ ❄️ **'FRIED' ONIONS**

Makes 1 pt/600 ml

2–3 large Spanish onions	*10–15 fl oz/300–450 ml chicken stock*

---

1   Peel the onions and cut them into wedges: eighths or six-teenths. Separate the pieces.
2   Combine the onions and 10–12 fl oz/300–360 ml of stock in a *heavy bottomed*, large frying pan (enamelled cast iron is best) that can be covered. Cover and bring to the boil. Let boil, covered, for 5–10 minutes, uncovering to stir very occasion-ally.
3   Uncover and reduce heat just a bit. When the onions are beginning to stick, pour in a splash of stock and stir and scrape well to loosen any browned bits on the bottom of the frying pan. Continue cooking and stirring for another minute or two, adding a splash of stock, and scraping to loosen the browned bits as necessary. When the onions are meltingly tender, amber brown and syrupy, they are ready.

'"Scheherazade! Scheherazade!" the king was calling. "Where shall I begin? I will peel the onions. We shall need hundreds and hundreds . . ."'

Wadeeha Atiyah, *Scheherazade Cooks*

Peppers

Because of their flavour, deep colour and luscious texture, yellow and red peppers are Slim Cuisine staples. To make the most of peppers, they must be peeled with a swivel-bladed vegetable peeler. Simply cut the peppers into their natural sections or cut them into strips and then peel each piece. The bonus of this peeling is that the peppers will become much more digestible as well as much more delicious and texturally interesting.

My secretary Rosemarie Espley – who is as adept at kitchen drill as at word processing – always gets the pepper-peeling detail when we are involved in demonstrations, and feeding large groups of people. She has peeled hundreds at a time. She advises that pepper peeling is a wonderful skin treatment; the pepper juices leave your hands soft and lovely. (Eat your heart out, Estée Lauder.)

Peppers may be peeled by two other methods as well: microwaving and grilling.

1   **To microwave.** ☐ Cut peppers in half, remove stems, seeds and ribs. Place 4 halves at a time, skin side down, on a paper towel on the microwave carousel. Microwave at full power for 3 minutes (yellow peppers) or 4 minutes (red peppers). Remove and let stand for 2 minutes. Strip the skins away with your fingers. Microwaved peppers are no longer raw, so use this method when you do not mind the loss of crispness. It will not work, for instance, for Marinated Peppers (page 136).
2   **To grill peppers.** Cut peppers in half. Remove core, ribs and seeds. Preheat the grill to high. Line the grill pan with foil, shiny side up. Place the peppers on the foil, skin side up. Push down to flatten slightly. Grill, until the peppers are blackened. Close the charred peppers in a bag. (Save any juices that have collected in the pan.) After 10 minutes, remove the peppers. Strip off the burnt skins and discard. This method produces *cooked* peppers. It has the added bonus of a pleasantly smoky taste.

Time Saving Tip: Good news – you can buy peeled red peppers in tins. They are labelled 'sweet red peppers' or 'pimientos'. Some of the tinned peppers have been grilled. When you are in a hurry you may substitute these for fresh peppers in any recipe that calls for the peppers to be cooked.

STIR-'FRIED' PEPPERS

Makes 2 pts/1200 ml

When I serve these at dinner parties, I get startled reactions. 'How *did* you prepare these peppers?', guests ask suspiciously as they gobble them down. They suspect the worst, that I have succumbed to the lure of butter and added a knob or two during the sautéing. I always offer these beauties as part of a Vegetable Selection (page 126). Eat as much as you like; despite the rich taste, the Calories are minimal, the fat is nil and the vitamins are just what you need.

---

3 red peppers	*6 fl oz/180 ml stock*
3 yellow peppers	*Freshly ground pepper to taste*

---

1   Cut the peppers in half, lengthwise. Remove the stem, the seeds and the ribs. Cut the halves into their natural sections.
2   Peel each pepper piece with a swivel-bladed vegetable peeler. Cut each piece into strips about ½ inch/1.25 cm wide.
3   Combine the peppers and the stock in a heavy frying pan. Grind in some black pepper and bring to the boil. When boiling, use two wooden spoons to toss and turn the peppers in the hot stock until the liquid has cooked down considerably. Turn down the heat a bit and 'fry' them for a few minutes in their own juices, until they are very tender, and the pepper juices have formed a thick sauce. Serve at once with their delicious juices. This dish may be made in advance and rewarmed later or the next day. It freezes well.

Dairy Products

Quark ♡ . It sounds like the cry of a drunken duck, a physicist will tell you that it is a sub-atomic particle, but food-lovers know that quark is a smooth, creamy, skimmed milk curd cheese. Several brands of quark are available throughout food stores in the UK; avoid those that list modified food starch in the ingredients. Quark is a superb cooking ingredient, and it is very good indeed spread on bread and toast.

Fromage Frais ♡ . Fromage frais is not as dense as quark. The texture is similar to that of soured cream or crème fraiche. Although it is called fromage – cheese – it is not particularly cheese-like. When you crave something creamy and rich, consider eating this exemplary dairy product right out of its container. Read the label – make sure you are buying fromage frais with less than

1% fat. How can anyone be depressed about a low-fat regime, with products like this to soothe and satisfy one's cravings?

Buttermilk ♡ . Buttermilk is as thick as cream, but it is cultured from skimmed milk. The taste is not *sour*, but pleasantly tangy. Buttermilk is an important ingredient in Slim Cuisine instant ice cream.

Mozzarella Cheese. Buy real Italian Mozzarella cheese, found in the dairy case of many supermarkets. It will be labelled 'part-skim' or 'medium fat', and will be packed in a liquid-filled pouch. Italian Mozzarella has a fresh, mild, milky taste, and melts like a dream.

Parmesan Cheese. Buy the real Italian stuff in a block, take it home and grate it. The easiest way to grate it is to cut it into smallish cubes and whirl them through the liquidizer. Parmesan cheese is a *medium*-fat cheese, so use it sparingly. You will find that a little goes a long way. Use pieces of the Parmesan rind to flavour soups and stews. Discard the rind when the dish is done.

'Well, I worked for him on that 101 inch aluminium line that he laid from Pennsylvania to California. We laid it to pipe buttermilk out to his camp out there. Paul [Bunyan] likes buttermilk so well himself that he had a twenty-four inch petcock running wide open all the time to catch enough for him to drink.'

Acel Garland, *Foller de Drinkin' Gou'd*

♡   Balsamic Vinegar

A magic ingredient if ever there was one. Balsamic vinegar is produced by boiling the must of Trebbiano di Spagno grapes until it thickens and caramelizes, then culturing it in wooden barrels. The flavour intensity, colour and quality of the vinegar is determined by the type of wood, the size of the barrel and the length of curing time. Good balsamic vinegar bears no resemblance to any other wine vinegar; the heady liquid is sweet-tasting, intense and mouth-filling. As it is, it makes a superb salad dressing, or a sauce for steamed vegetables, potatoes, fish, or meats. Because I don't eat salad dressing or sauces in restaurants (they contain too much fat), I depend on the pocket flask of balsamic vinegar that I carry with me all the time. My husband (brilliant and considerate man that he is) gave me the flask for my birthday, and keeps it topped up with a good balsamic vinegar. I get odd looks in restaurants when I pull out my flask and flourish it over naked salads and vegetables, but it makes low-fat restaurant meals positively luxurious. And – of course – it's a great conversation piece. Orso's, one of my favourite London restaurants, uses balsamic vinegar in several dishes, and – if you ask – will actually put a large bottle of the nectar on your table, so that you can pour at will. How tempted I have been to pull out my flask and a siphon, or even to pour it into my wine glass and quaff it down. But civilized behaviour always wins in the end and I confine myself to pouring it liberally over everything in sight.

♡ # Sun-Dried Tomatoes

In America, they say that sun-dried tomatoes are the ketchup of the eighties. Wait until you taste them! Leathery, with a dark, intense, over-the-top ripe tomato flavour, they are quite irresistible, and add wonderful depth to sauces, soups and stews. Sun-dried tomatoes are now available dry pack (no oil), so you can eat yourself silly on them, and use them freely in recipes. The ones from Italy are slightly salty, the ones from the United States are not. They are not budget food, but why not count up the money you are saving by *not* buying butter, crisps, cigarettes, sweet bars, fish-and-chip takeaways, vegetable oil, and so on. Invest some of those healthy savings on sybaritic, healthy treats. Sun-dried tomatoes and balsamic vinegar help to make a low-fat lifestyle a culinary dream.

♡ # Soy Sauce/Teriyaki Sauce

Either of these Oriental products (they can be found in virtually every supermarket) can be used as part of the 'Holy Trinity' of low-fat mushroom cookery (see page 22). They should be used sparingly because their salt content is high. You probably won't want to add additional salt to any recipe using either sauce. People who must confine themselves to a low-salt regime will find balsamic vinegar (page 26) an excellent substitute.

♡ # Dried Mushrooms

Dried *Boletus edulis* mushrooms (called porcini in Italy, cèpes in France) and dried Chinese or Japanese mushrooms (shiitakes) are available in delicatessens, speciality food halls and some super-markets. An ounce/30 grams of dried mushrooms goes a long way, and can give low-fat cookery an enormous flavour boost. When reconstituted, dried mushrooms plump up to at least five times their dried weight. The flavour, then, will be up to twenty times as intense as that of an ounce/30 grams of the same mushroom in its undried (fresh) state.

Dried mushrooms harbour quantities of sand and grit in their nooks and crannies. Always rinse them well in *cold* water before reconstituting. After soaking ½–1 hour, rinse them again and strain the soaking water through a coffee filter, or doubled cheese cloth. *Never* discard the strained soaking water; it is a rich essence of mushroom and should be used in the dish being prepared, or frozen to enrich future soups, stews and sauces.

Larder and Freezer Staples

Frozen Vegetables and Fruit. Commercially frozen vegetables can be terrific. Not all of them. Frozen asparagus is a travesty of the real thing, frozen broccoli and frozen potatoes are pretty grim, frozen courgettes, mushrooms and cauliflower are terrible. But frozen sweetcorn, peas, button sprouts, diced swedes: it's hard to imagine doing without them. Frozen fruits, too, make one's cooking life so much easier. They are incredibly useful in all sorts of recipes, and their taste and quality involve *no* compromise. One of the best kitchen investments you can make is in a big chest freezer. If you keep your eye on the classifieds in your local paper, you may find a good bargain in a used freezer. Security is having a freezer full of high-quality staples, so that when a cooking frenzy strikes, the raw ingredients are there, waiting in suspended animation.

Tinned Vegetables. There are several tinned vegetables that are so useful and good tasting that you should never be without them.

Artichoke hearts
Sweet red peppers (pimientos)
Italian tomatoes
Broad beans
Red kidney beans and white ones (cannelini)
Borlotti beans and black-eyed beans
Chick peas
Chillies (jalapeños and green chillies)

'One of my chief pleasures in life was dealing with store bought food – all so virginally packaged yet bursting to be opened.'

Lucy Ellman, *Sweet Desserts*

28

Meals for Special Occasions

'Each succeeding course must lead to new ecstasy, else will
the dinner turn out the worst of failures.'

Elizabeth Robins Pennell, *A Guide for the Greedy
by a Greedy Woman*

Liberated Sunday Lunch

Where I come from, people eat brunch on Sunday. It begins at 12-ish with Mimosas (champagne mixed with fresh orange juice) or Bloody Mary Soup (vodka mixed with piquant tomato juice, served up in a soup plate with a generous sprinkling of fresh herbs, chopped chillies and a *large* soup spoon). The liquid refreshment is usually followed by poached or scrambled eggs, and bagels thickly spread with cream cheese, draped with smoked salmon, and topped with ruby red slices of ripe tomato and slivers of sweet onion. Coleslaw, potato salad, Greek black olives, Danish pastry and cup after cup of strong black coffee complete the New York Sunday ritual. It's a casual and very relaxed meal – someone runs out for the Sunday papers (someone strong – the Sunday *New York Times* is bigger than all the English Sunday papers *put together!*), someone else nips out to the corner deli to pick up the bagels, salads, smoked salmon and Danish pastry, and everyone lazes around in comfortable old clothes.

When we arrived in England, invitations flooded in from new friends for Sunday lunch. Sunday after Sunday, we sat at formal tables, in our good clothes, and consumed roast leg of lamb, roast potatoes, huge plates of vegetables and profound puddings, only to stagger home in the evening replete and bemused by our sudden departure from our old Sunday brunch habits.

I must say that the traditional English Sunday lunch is festive and tasty, but its major flaw, other than its ridiculously high fat and Calorie count, is that it reduces the cook (usually the woman of the house) – the poor slave responsible for the orchestration of the epic production – to the status of a drudge, madly trying to organize a complicated and labour-intensive meal on what should be a relaxing day off. For the one who prepares it, Sunday lunch can be nightmarishly exhausting. The elaborate several-course meal turns mother into a whirling dervish in the centre of a hysterical flurry of flashing knives, roaring kitchen machines and blasting cookers. When the food – painstakingly choreographed so that each component is done at the same time – is finally prepared, the cook slumps at the table, almost too tired to lift fork to mouth, but the slump doesn't last long. She must bounce up and down like a manic yo-yo, replenishing plates with extra servings, filling glasses, clearing dishes away, rushing in the pudding, pouring coffee . . . and when it's all over, and the relaxed family nod off over the paper and the telly, she must face the shambolic kitchen.

Do yourself a favour and rethink Sunday lunch. I'm offering

suggestions on two points: (1) how to cut down on the frightening fat and Calorie count, and (2) how to cut down on the drudgery. Enjoy the ritual and delicious Sunday family food, but make it healthy, relaxing and festive for *all*, even the cook.

SUNDAY LUNCH MENU

Braised Brisket of Beef (page 68) *or* Pot Roast Lamb (page 73)
Roast Potatoes (page 132)
Braised Carrots (page 124)
Whipped Swedes (page 128)
Fruit Compôte (page 147) or Bread Pudding (page 150)

'Every Sunday, everyone got stoned on dinner except the women who cooked it and thereby lost their appetites – the rest of us did our duty and ate ourselves into a gaseous stupor and sat around in a trance and mumbled like a bunch of beefheads.'

Garrison Keillor, *Lake Wobegon Days*

DRUDGERY BEGONE!

My liberated Sunday lunch gives a choice of two joints: a brisket of beef or a leg of lamb.

Brisket is a remarkable cut of beef. Boned and mercilessly trimmed of fat (see pages 66–7 for specific instructions), it cooks for hours unattended, and emerges from the oven buttery tender. The gravy is spectacularly rich and deeply flavoured, although virtually fat-free after you've skimmed it. The brisket may be completely prepared as much as 3 days before you plan to serve it. Indeed, it tastes even better when it has mellowed in the refrigerator for a day or so. The leg of lamb is marinated first in a mixture of wine, tomatoes and spices. This marination can be done as early as two days ahead of time. On Sunday morning, once the joint is put into the oven, it is unattended except for basting after the first hour.

The whipped swedes can be prepared days ahead of time, and refrigerated or frozen. They reheat from frozen in the microwave with no loss of quality. If your oven has a grill compartment that doubles as an extra oven, use it to roast the carrots and potatoes while the joints cook. Once they are in the oven, they need not be fussed over. If you have no extra oven compartment, roast them along with the joint. Because the oven temperature will be lower than what is called for in the recipe, leave them in for longer than specified. The carrots can be trimmed and peeled and arranged in a baking dish the night before, or early in the morning. The stock in the potato recipe can be poured into a baking dish and refrigerated the night before or early morning as well. Cut and add the potatoes on Sunday just before roasting.

All these things can roast happily together with minimal interference from the cook, and they fill the house with delicious Sunday smells.

Both puddings are do-ahead ones: the compôte can be made days ahead – the longer it mellows the better it tastes. The bread pudding can be assembled on the day before, and then cooked while the family eat the joint and vegetables, or it can be assembled the morning before, baked in the evening, and cooled and refrigerated. Bring it out of the fridge early enough on Sunday for it to be at room temperature when served.

Barbecues and Picnics

Picnics during daylight hours have a nutritional importance that goes beyond the food. There are four 'fat-soluble' vitamins, vitamins A, E, K and D. These vitamins are generally found associated with fatty or oily foods. People existing on very low fat diets have no problem with vitamin A if they eat food rich in beta-carotene (see page 4); our bodies can use the beta-carotene to manufacture plenty of the vitamin.

Our bodies' need for vitamin E is tied to the amount of unsaturated fat we ingest. The less fat consumed, the less vitamin E needed. And vitamin E, along with K and A, is readily available in whole grains, meat and leafy greens – important components of Slim Cuisine, so no problem exists. But vitamin D is another story. In fact, it may not be a vitamin at all, since it is not readily available in natural foods but can be manufactured in the body. In England, butter and margarine are artificially fortified with D. When you cut these foods out, you also cut out your dietary source of the vitamin. Of course, to get the full daily requirement of D it would be necessary to eat more than 1200 Calories of margarine a day, or 9000 Calories of butter – not a desirable or healthy practice. But expose yourself to sunlight, and your body, that exquisite organic machine, manufactures plenty of vitamin D, and you never have to give butter or margarine another thought. That doesn't mean that you have to strip naked and fling yourself on the ground to grill for hours under a relentless, blazing sun. Normal exposure in everyday clothing is fine, even in a country like England, that feels so grey most of the time. People who compulsively cover themselves – arms, faces and all – and never venture out of doors may develop vitamin D deficiency, but these cases are rare.

How pleasant to bolster your vitamin D by eating out of doors every once in a while, even on partly cloudy days. Just remember, when holidaying in sunny climes, or enjoying a rare English heatwave, there is no need to overdo it. *Over*exposure to sunlight results in wrinkles and possible skin cancer.

BARBECUE MENU

Beetroot Borscht (page 56)
Vegetable Canapés (page 38)
Grilled Goose Skirt Steak (page 67)
Spicy Potato Salad (page 135)
Oranges with Orange Brandy (page 157)

PICNIC MENU

Gazpacho (page 55)
Stuffed Mushrooms (page 38)
Chicken Pesto Potato Salad (page 93)
Strawberries in Raspberry Sauce (page 141)

Breakfast

There is something appealing about a large breakfast; huge platters of steaming food, ending the long fast of the preceding night, and stoking the body and brain for the onslaught of a new and vigorous work day. But the traditional English breakfast carries things too far. Sausages, potatoes, eggs, mushrooms, and so on, are undoubtedly marvellous, but oh! the rivulets of grease, the sputtering fat, the lashings of butter, the downright lardiness of it all. Why not enjoy the wonderfully strength-giving glories of an English breakfast minus the fat dimension? The tastes of the good ingredients, without their usual blunting veil of grease, will delight you.

What a lovely way to start the day!

'Today's the day I'm gonna do it. Today's the day I'm gonna go on a diet . . . I gotta have will power – I gotta be strong . . . So make me a big breakfast 'cause I got to have a lot of strength to go with this diet.'

Sid Caesar, a monologue from *Your Show of Shows*

SLIM CUISINE VERSION OF TRADITIONAL ENGLISH 'FRY-UP' BREAKFAST

Poached Egg (Eat eggs only occasionally – the yolks contain fat. And if your blood cholesterol levels are high, avoid them altogether.)

Pan-'Fried' Potatoes with Onions (page 130)
Pan-'Fried' Mushrooms (page 22, use whole button mushrooms)
Grilled Tomatoes (halve tomatoes and cook under the grill)
Baked Beans (use the kind that are made with no sugar or fat)
Breakfast Sausage Patties (page 84)
Toasted Wholemeal Bread with Plum Jam (page 140)

Although I have specifically decided *not* to include Calorie and fat counts in this book (see page 12), I could not resist hauling out the tables and computing levels for the good old English breakfast. The following chart is a dramatic example of Calorie and fat savings possible using Slim Cuisine techniques. A full Slim Cuisine breakfast instead of a traditional one will save you 666 Calories and 56.1 grams of fat.

Total Calories and Fat

Slim Cuisine Style			**Traditional Style**	
Calories	*fat (g)*		*Calories*	*fat (g)*
78	5.5	Poached/Fried Egg	210	20.2
171	0.5	Pan-'Fried' Potatoes	450	20.0
7	0.0	Mushrooms	20	2.0
20	0.0	Grilled Tomatoes	20	0.0
54	0.0	Baked Beans	72	0.0
20	0.2	Breakfast Sausage	94	8.8
55	0.7	Wholemeal Toast	55	0.7
00	0.0	Butter per tablespoon	102	11.3
11	0.0	Plum Jam per tablespoon	59	0.0
416	6.9		1082	63.0

'She says that she will be his if he renounces his lust for treasure and saturated fats.'

Tom Weller, *Cvltvre made Stvpid*

QUICK BREAKFASTS

Not everyone can face a heaped plate of hot food early in the day. And many people lack the time even to consider a labour-intensive kitchen production at the start of a work day. What a shame though, to forgo breakfast entirely because of such restriction. Try one of the following quickies to give your day a good nutritional and psychological boost.

Traditional New York Breakfast

Bagels halved, and then each half spread with quark or Chive Spread (page 46). Lay on each a slice of smoked salmon, a slice of ripe tomato and a few slivers of Spanish onion.

Cereal

Small shredded wheats or other cereal that has no added fat or sugar, mixed with berries or sliced fruit, dribbled with skimmed milk.

Cheese-Lover's Breakfast

Toasted rye or wholemeal bread with a thin slice or two of low-fat Italian Mozzarella cheese. Grill until the Cheese is melted, bubbly and lightly speckled with brown.

Fish-Lover's Breakfast ⑤

Quark or fromage frais and flaked smoked mackerel blended until smooth in a food processor. If you wish, blend in some chopped chives and a drop or two of lemon juice. Serve spread on toasted rye, granary, or wholemeal bread.

Christmas

In January, every women's magazine devotes itself to low-Calorie cookery advice, every publisher releases the newest crop of weight loss books, every newspaper offers wisdom on healthy eating, and almost everyone gets down to some serious dieting. Why? Because December is the month in which *everyone*, even reformed fatoholics, succumb to temptation. All the fat-lined pitfalls are there to ensnare you: over-the-top family dinners; office parties and cock-tail gatherings with unlimited supplies of free booze and fatty, sugary nibbles; traditional eggnogs; stuffed geese and turkeys; fruit cakes; suet puddings; mince pies; brandy butter; potatoes roasted in dripping; butter-bathed vegetables; oil-drenched salads. Mayonnaise – lard – chicken fat – olive oil. Clotted cream – whipped cream – double cream – soured cream. It's enough to drive one literally insane with fat overkill.

'Near the Eastern Horizon the sky was the colour of chicken livers simmering in butter. Flocks of birds melted against the sunrise in chocolate tones.'

Scott Sanders, *The Artist of Hunger*

I am one thin voice calling out in the December fat jungle. Please listen. *You don't have to succumb.* The police will not show up at your

35

door to haul you away to the clink if you refuse to bake the traditional mince pies this year. Nowhere in the Bible is it commanded that you glut yourself or your family with fat on the day set aside to honour Christ's birth. If you eschew the salted nuts, the brandy butter, the fruit cake, the chipolatas, a bolt of lightning will not plunge through your roof to scorch you to cinders. If you play down the Dickensian excess, your citizenship will not be snatched from you. Chances are you do not want to fall into the fat-lined pit, in fact you probably long – with all your heart – to avoid it. *Do* so. Be the master of your own destiny. If the booze and fattening food are undulating and pulsating all around you, *you don't have to consume them.*

I have learned this over the years, but it can be difficult. At a gala banquet at one of the Cambridge Colleges an eminent nutrition professor seated on my left accused me of anorexia because I refused the rack of lamb (nestled as it was in half an inch of its own fat), took only the vegetables that were not swimming in butter and cream sauce, passed on the salad dressing, quaffed mineral water and ended my meal with naked raspberries. This is not anorexia, Professor; this is common sense, good taste and self-protection. Let them call you anorexic, heartless, a goody-goody, or an ascetic – it doesn't matter. You are the master of your own destiny, and January will find you beautifully slim, healthy and laughing up your perfectly fitting sleeve at the rest of the chubby population.

SLIM CUISINE CHRISTMAS MENU

There is nothing spartan or dietetic-tasting about this menu. You will need to make no apologies. Everyone will feel beautifully and festively fed, but they will not hate themselves in the morning.

Vegetable Canapés (page 38)
Chicken Liver Pâté (page 41)
Roast Turkey (page 87)
Chestnut Stuffing (page 88)
Sausage Patties (page 84)
Spicy Sprouts (page 128)
Purée of Swede, Turnip and White Beans (page 129)
Cauliflower and Peppers (page 122)
Roast Potatoes (page 132)
Mince Pies (page 150) or Mincemeat Bread Pudding with Lemon
    Cream Sauce (pages 149 and 151)
Black and White Meringues (page 146)
Oranges in Orange Brandy (page 157)

Starters, Spreads and Snacks

'There is no love sincerer than the love of food.'
George Bernard Shaw, *Man and Superman*

VEGETABLE CANAPÉS

An array of chicory leaves, mushroom caps and varying-coloured pepper boats, filled with vivid (in flavour as well as hue) stuffings, makes a stunning first course for a special dinner party or buffet. It provides an almost over-the-top feast for the eyes, titillates the palate with fresh and exhilarating tastes, and gives the diners something to talk about. If you don't want to fiddle about with teaspoons ('Life is too short to stuff a mushroom', and all that), pile each filling into a separate glass bowl, place on a platter, and surround with lavish heaps of multi-coloured pepper pieces, mushroom caps and chicory leaves. It will still be delicious, visually beautiful and a conversation starter. Along with the fillings suggested below, you might want to add Beetroot Purée and Jellied Gazpacho (double the amount of gelatine called for) from *Slim Cuisine I*.

½ lb/240 g small button
    mushrooms
3 fl oz/90 ml vegetable stock
3 fl oz/90 ml dry white wine or dry
    white vermouth
2 dashes soy sauce
Chicory heads

Peppers (a combination of red,
    green, yellow, purple – whatever
    you can find)
Herb Fillings (see page 39)
Pesto (see page 17)
Red Pepper and Garlic Spread (see
    page 45)
Mock Guacamole (see page 44)

---

1   Carefully remove the stems from the mushroom caps. Save the stems for another use. With a teaspoon, gently even out the mushroom cap opening so it will hold a filling nicely.
2   Pour the stock, vermouth and soy sauce into a non-stick frying pan that will hold the mushroom caps in one layer. Bring the liquid to the boil. Add the mushroom caps in one layer, stem side up, reduce heat, and simmer for 2–3 minutes. Raise heat and cook, tossing the mushrooms in the pan for a few minutes, until the caps are cooked but still quite firm, and the liquid is reduced and syrupy. Remove from the pan, drain upside down on paper towels.
3   Slice off the core of the chicory heads and separate the leaves. Rinse and dry.
4   Stem and seed peppers and derib. Cut into 'boats' about 1 inch/2.5 cm long.
5   With a teaspoon, fill each mushroom cap. Put a teaspoonful of filling at the base of each chicory leaf. Fill each pepper boat. Arrange on a beautiful plate.

Herb Fillings

---

1 pt/600 ml very low fat yoghurt
Chopped fresh mint
Chopped fresh basil

Chopped fresh parsley or fresh
coriander

Divide the yoghurt into three parts. Stir the mint into one, the basil into the second and the parsley or coriander into the third. Refrigerate until needed.

Filo Pastry

Filo (sometimes spelt 'phyllo') or strudel, tissue-thin sheets of delicate pastry, are available frozen from some supermarkets and delicatessens. Some brands contain no fat at all, one brand contains a very small percentage of corn oil – not enough to preclude your using the versatile stuff when you suffer pastry cravings. The traditional method of handling this dough involves layering the thin sheets, and brushing each layer with butter or oil, thus forming a many-layered, crispy finished pastry. I've substituted egg white for the butter and oil. As a result the nature of the pastry changes; it is more like a tender yeast dough than a brittle strudel or a mille-feuille.

Filo is fun, and easy to work with; just follow the directions exactly, and you should have no problems. If not cosseted, the sheets dry out quickly and turn into a parchment-like, brittle substance that disintegrates at a touch, hence the instructions for covering with greaseproof paper and a damp cloth. Many people have asked me how they can have pastry on the Slim Cuisine regime. Here is the answer. Enjoy it to your heart's content. (See also the Mince Pie recipe on page 150.)

 LAMB SAMOSA

1 box of filo makes 12 samosas

The lamb mixture is also good as a pâté; a sort of spiced lamb rillettes. Chill it in ceramic ramekins, and serve with wedges of split, toasted pitta bread. Leftover lamb filling freezes very well.

Lamb Filling

2 medium onions, chopped
2 cloves garlic, minced
1 thin slice peeled ginger, minced
2 lb/960 g lean minced lamb
Salt to taste
1 teaspoon turmeric
1½ teaspoons ground coriander
¼ teaspoon red pepper flakes
Pinch of cayenne pepper

1 teaspoon cinnamon
½ teaspoon cardamom
½ teaspoon allspice
4 fl oz/120 ml stock
2 tablespoons tomato paste
1 Baked Aubergine, peeled and
  chopped (see page 21)
1 tablespoon garam masala

1   Combine onions, garlic, ginger and lamb in a wide heavy frying pan. Cook slowly until the lamb is thoroughly cooked. Break up the meat with a wooden spoon as it cooks. Drain in a colander over a bowl to drain away all fat. Blot the meat with paper towels to eliminate even more fat. Blot the frying pan. Return meat and onion mixture to the frying pan.

2   Add the spices from salt through allspice to the meat. Cook and stir over low heat until the meat is coated with the spices. Stir in stock, tomato paste, aubergine and garam masala. Simmer, partially covered, for about 30 minutes, until thick. Set aside. (At this point it can be refrigerated for 2–3 days.)

Pastry

1 package frozen filo pastry

Place the filo pastry in the refrigerator to thaw the night before you want to use it. It can stay in the refrigerator for up to 2 days.

To Assemble

Thawed filo
2–3 egg whites, lightly beaten

Lamb filling

1   Preheat oven to 375° F, 190° C, Gas Mark 5.

2   Put a barely damp tea towel on your work surface. Cover it with a sheet of waxed paper or greaseproof paper. Unwrap the filo, unfold it and place it on the paper. From top to bottom, with a sharp knife, cut the stack of pastry down the centre. Immediately cover the stack with another sheet of waxed or greaseproof paper and then with another barely damp tea towel.

3 Take one piece of filo from the stack. Keep the rest well covered. Spread the sheet out on a clean surface. With a pastry brush, lightly coat it with egg white. Fold the bottom third up and then the top third down as if folding a business letter. Place a generous tablespoon of filling on the lower right-hand corner. Fold down to form a triangle. Brush with egg white. Fold back up to form a new triangle. Brush with egg white. Continue folding and brushing lightly until you have formed a compact, many-layered triangle. (See diagram below.) Brush the finished triangle lightly with egg white and place on a *non-stick* baking dish. (At this point, the samosas may be refrigerated for a day or two, or frozen for months.)

4 Bake the samosas in the oven for 20–30 minutes, or until puffed up and golden. If baking from frozen, add an extra 5 minutes to the baking time. Serve at once.

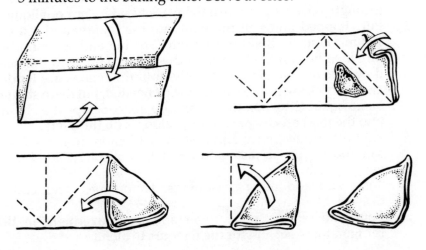

♡ ❄ Variation: Vegetable Samosa

Follow directions above, substituting Couscous with Vegetables (page 101) or Vegetable Curry (*Slim Cuisine I*) for the lamb mix.

Ⓢ CHICKEN LIVER PÂTÉ

Makes approximately 32 fl oz/960 ml

My favourite piece of ill-conceived menu prose comes from somewhere in the hinterlands of the American South: 'Chef's own Liver Pâté'. Talk about throwing oneself into one's work! This recipe should by rights be called 'Annie's own Liver Pâté', because I've adapted it from a recipe developed by my friend Dr Ann Coxon.

The pâté has a silken texture. As you feel it roll voluptuously over your tongue, you'll also feel pangs of guilt; it tastes wickedly fattening. But have no fear. High nutrition, minimal fat – isn't life wonderful?

1¼ lb/600 g chicken livers,
 trimmed
Approximately 8 fl oz/240 ml stock
1 onion, chopped
3 tablespoons brandy
30 pitted prunes, soaked in water
 for an hour or so and drained

Juice and zest of 1–2 large lemons
14 fl oz/420 ml fromage frais
Salt and freshly ground pepper to
 taste
Pinch or two of allspice

---

1   Film a non-stick frying pan with a tiny bit of stock. Sauté chicken livers in one layer in the pan until they are *just* cooked through. (Use tongs to turn them.) Set aside. Pour out liquid.
2   Put chopped onion in the pan with the brandy and 4 fl oz/120 ml of stock. Boil for 1 minute, stirring and scraping the browned bits on the bottom of the frying pan. Turn the heat down, cover and simmer briskly until the onions are tender and amber brown. Add more stock if needed, but there should be no liquid left when the onions are done. Scrape the onions into the food processor container along with the livers.
3   Add the prunes, juice and zest from 1 lemon, fromage frais, salt and pepper to taste and a pinch of allspice. Blend until very smooth.
4   Taste and add more seasonings, lemon juice and zest if desired. Blend again.
5   Pour into ceramic pots, cover and leave overnight in the refrigerator to set and for the flavours to blend.

Note: Chicken livers are low in fat, high in vitamins and minerals, but high in cholesterol as well. If your blood cholesterol levels are high, do not eat liver of any kind.

NACHOS

Nachos – little corn chips topped with tomatoes and cheese – are irresistible. I defy you to eat just one. (Or just two, for that matter.) These compelling morsels make great party food.

Tortillas (see page 98)
Tomato Sauce (page 16) or
   Tomato-Pepper Sauce (see
   page 80)
Italian Mozzarella cheese, cut into
   strips

Dried oregano
Freshly ground pepper
Fresh coriander leaves (optional)
Fromage frais

1   Preheat oven to 300° F, 150° C, Gas Mark 2.
2   Bake tortillas directly on the oven shelf, turning once, for
    15–20 minutes until crisp right through. (Test by breaking
    one. It should break with a crisp 'snap'.) Break each tortilla
    into eights. They will keep, in a covered tin, for months (if you
    hide them).
3   Preheat the grill. Spread the tortilla chips, in one layer, on a
    foil-lined baking sheet. Put a dollop of sauce on each. Top with
    a strip of Mozzarella cheese. Sprinkle on some oregano (rub it
    between your fingertips), and grind on some pepper.
4   Grill, about 3 inches/8 cm) from the heat, until the cheese is
    melted, approximately 3 minutes. Transfer the nachos to a
    plate and garnish with coriander leaves if desired. Serve at
    once. Pass a bowl of fromage frais so that each diner may
    garnish each nacho with a dollop.

Variation I: Potato Skin Nachos

When you have scooped out baked jacket potatoes in order to make
Mashed Potatoes (see page 108), *do not throw the skins away!* Save
them, wrapped in foil in the fridge, until the snack urge strikes,
then make Potato Skin Nachos. Cut the skins into 2 inch/5 cm
squares. Place in one layer, skin-side down, on a foil-lined baking
tray. Grill, 3 inches/8 cm from the heat, for 30–40 seconds, to crisp a
bit. Then spoon a dollop of sauce on each, top with a strip of
Mozzarella, sprinkle with oregano and cook and serve as above.

Variation II: Tortilla Pizzas

My 17-year-old son Shawm, the teenage pizza monster, invented
this method. Open a tin of tortillas. Insert two into the toaster slots.
Toast until crisp through. (Watch it – they should not brown or
burn. It won't take very long. Underestimate the time and then
push them back down if necessary. Timing depends on your
particular toaster.) Place the whole, crisp tortillas on a foil-
lined baking tray. Sprinkle with shredded Mozzarella. Grill for
approximately 3 minutes. Serve at once.

ARTICHOKE TOASTS

Makes approximately 15 pieces

A crisp bread base with a rich creamy topping laced with artichoke pieces. Artichoke toasts are ridiculously easy to prepare, but they make an impressive party nibble.

---

4 fl oz/120 ml fromage frais
½ tablespoon Dijon mustard
1 tin artichoke hearts, drained and
  chopped
1 tablespoon grated Parmesan
  cheese

Dash or two Tabasco sauce
1 medium baguette, about
  10 inches/25 cm long, split
Freshly ground pepper

---

1   Preheat grill.
2   Whisk together fromage frais and mustard in a bowl. Stir in the chopped artichoke hearts, Parmesan cheese and Tabasco sauce.
3   Spread this mixture on the cut sides of the two baguette halves. Grill, 3 inches/8 cm from the heat, until browned, approximately 3 minutes. Cut into 1–1½ inch/2.5–4 cm slices, place on a plate, and serve.

♡ Omit cheese.

♡ 🧸 ⏲ ⑤ MOCK GUACAMOLE (MONTEZUMA'S MUSHY PEAS)

Makes 1 pt/600 ml

I wish I had invented this brilliant recipe. I've adapted it from *Secret Ingredients* by Michael Roberts, an enthusiastic and innovative (to say the least) American chef. Guacamole is an ancient Mexican classic: ripe avocados, chillies and onions ground to a rough purée in a *molcajete* (a mortar carved from volcanic rock). Modern city-bred Mexican cooks use electric liquidizers to make the rough green paste (they affectionately refer to the *molcajete*, still in use in rural areas, as the 'liquidora Azteca'), but the resulting guacamole is the same as it has been for many centuries. I once served guacamole to an ethnobotanist who had earned his graduate degree in Mexico. 'Montezuma would have recognized this,' he mused, as he scooped a bit more of the vivid and spicy mixture on to a tortilla chip. His comment gave me a giddy feeling of timelessness, as if I were about to trade recipes with Montezuma himself. But times change. Avocados are very high in fat Calories, and have

44

no place in Slim Cuisine, hence my devotion to this odd recipe, a kind of cross between guacamole and mushy peas. Odd it may be (Montezuma would laugh me out of the kitchen), but it is also absolutely splendid; one of the freshest, zingiest mixtures imaginable.

2–3 fl oz/60–90 ml fresh coriander leaves	*1 lb/480 g defrosted frozen peas*
2 tablespoons lime juice	*¼ teaspoon ground cumin*
1 fresh chilli pepper, seeded and coarsely diced	*Salt to taste*
	¼ medium red onion, diced

1 Place coriander, lime juice and chilli in the jar of the liquidizer or food processor. Process until coarsely chopped.
2 Add peas, cumin and salt and blend to a rough purée. Scrape into a bowl and stir in the onion. Serve with tortilla chips, toasted split pitta bread wedges, or motzah crackers.

♡ ⑤ RED PEPPER AND GARLIC SPREAD

Makes 16 fl oz/480 ml

I devised this while trying to work out a substitute for rouille, the red pepper and garlic mayonnaise of the South of France. If you want a really strong garlicky taste, add a crushed clove or two of fresh garlic, but I prefer the mellow and subtle character of the whole roasted bulb.

Purée from 1 head Baked Garlic (see page 17)	*Several dashes Tabasco sauce*
1 large tin pimientos (red peppers), drained	*1 lb/480 g quark*

Combine all ingredients in a liquidizer or food processor and blend until smooth. Serve as a dip, a spread, a filling for Vegetable Canapés (page 38), or an accompaniment to fish soups and stews.

⊕   Roast garlic in the microwave.

Slim Sandwiches

Legend has it that the Fourth Earl of Sandwich, unwilling to leave the gaming table although quite hungry, invented a portable meal. Did he have any inkling of the culinary revolution he was setting in motion? How could he envisage baked beans on toast, chip butties, stuffed pittas, bagels and cream cheese, hamburgers, ham and swiss, hot dogs, peanut butter and jelly? That impromptu eighteenth-century portable meal, in all its twentieth-century guises, now bears the Earl's name. There is no other meal that offers such a contrast of flavours and textures in a single bite. In fact, a sandwich makes a happy occasion. Two pieces of bread and an interesting filling can add glamour to any lunch box, and cheer a gloomy mood. In your quest for great sandwiches, don't fall into the butter and mayonnaise trap. Spread your sandwiches with quark or any of the quark spreads from this collection or from *Slim Cuisine I*. Try Red Pepper and Garlic Spread, Pesto, Chive Spread – even 'Russian' Dressing (substitute quark for the fromage frais and cut down on the buttermilk).

♡ ⊕ ⑤ **CHIVE SPREAD**

Makes 6 fl oz/180 ml

A prime example of how quark can be used to make excellent rich-tasting spreads for bread. To turn this into a garlic spread, substitute Baked Garlic purée (page 17) for the chives. The chive spread is particularly good on split bagels or brown bread, topped with slices of smoked salmon.

---

1 box (7 oz/210 g) quark
1 bunch fresh chives

---

1   Scrape the quark into the bowl of a food processor. With scissors, snip the chives over the bowl, so the pieces fall in.
2   Process until the quark is very smooth, creamy and green-flecked. Scrape into a ramekin or small bowl, cover with cling film and refrigerate until needed.

Soups

'"Have some soup," Lizzie said. "Soup is good for stress."'
Marsha Norman, *The Fortune Teller*

♡ 🧸 🕐 LETTUCE AND FENNEL SOUP

Makes 1½ pts/900 ml

This recipe was given to me by Tony Smith, the proprietor of the Mange Tout Bistro in Norwich. The soup's creamy richness comes from the eponymous vegetables.

---

1 large iceberg (crisphead) lettuce	*16 fl oz/480 ml stock*
3 bulbs fennel, trimmed (save the feathery leaves) and coarsely chopped	*Salt and freshly ground pepper to taste*
	Fromage frais

---

1   Chop the head of lettuce into chunks. Cook it slowly in a heavy-bottomed pot. When juices begin to form, add the fennel.
2   Let the vegetables sauté in their own juices until tender, about 20 minutes, stirring occasionally.
3   Stir in the stock and season to taste. Simmer for 5 minutes more.
4   Purée the soup in the liquidizer. Serve hot, with a dollop of fromage frais and a sprig of fennel leaves on each serving.

♡ ❄ RED PEPPER AND TOMATO BORSCHT

Makes 4 pts/2400 ml

What a heavenly brew; a really wild improvisation on a classic theme. The borscht fairly bursts with flavour, texture and nutrition. It freezes beautifully. A container pulled from the freezer, thawed and reheated in the microwave and served with good crusty bread makes a sumptuous meal.

---

2 large Spanish onions, chopped	*1 large tin (1 lb 12 oz/840 g) plum tomatoes, drained and chopped*
1 small carrot, peeled and chopped	
1 medium baking potato, peeled and coarsely chopped	*1 tablespoon sultanas*
2½ pts/1500 ml stock	*1 tablespoon brown sugar*
8 large red peppers, trimmed, ribbed, seeded and coarsely diced	*1 tablespoon lemon juice*
	1 heaped tablespoon tomato paste
Salt and freshly ground pepper to taste	*1 tablespoon chopped parsley*
5 shallots, coarsely chopped	*Purée from ½–1 large head Baked Garlic (see page 17)*

Grated zest of half a small lemon
3 oz/90 g chopped sun-dried
    tomatoes
1 teaspoon red wine vinegar
8 fl oz/240 ml red wine
½ teaspoon allspice

1 small cabbage (8–10 oz/240–
    300 g), cored, trimmed of tough
    outer leaves and shredded
Veal-Potato Balls (see page 81)
Fromage frais
Fresh dill fronds

---

1   Combine onions, carrot, potato and 4 fl oz/120 ml stock in a soup pot. Cover and bring to the boil. Reduce heat and simmer briskly for 3–4 minutes. Uncover and cook, stirring occasionally, until the liquid is gone, and the vegetables are browning. Stir in the peppers.

2   Pour in the remaining stock. Season with a bit of salt and pepper. Simmer, partially covered, for ½ hour, or until the vegetables are very tender. Set aside to cool.

3   While the soup is simmering, combine the shallots, lemon zest, sun-dried tomatoes, vinegar and wine in a frying pan. Cover and bring to the boil. Uncover and boil until the wine has evaporated. Cook, stirring, on moderate heat until the shallots are tender.

4   Remove from heat and add allspice. Stir to coat vegetables. Stir in the remaining ingredients except cabbage, Veal-Potato Balls, fromage frais and dill. Simmer, uncovered, until thick. Set aside.

5   Purée the cooled pepper mixture in the blender, in batches, and then push through a sieve. The pepper skins will be left behind. Discard them. Combine the sieved pepper mixture and the tomato mixture in the soup pot. Add the cabbage. Thin with more broth if necessary. Simmer, partially covered, for 20 minutes, until the cabbage is almost tender.

6   Add the Veal-Potato Balls. Simmer, partially covered, for 10 minutes, to blend flavours and to finish the cabbage. Taste and adjust seasonings, adding salt, pepper, lemon juice and brown sugar, as needed. The soup should have a nice balance of sweet and sour. If possible, refrigerate for a day or so to mellow.

7   To serve, heat until piping hot. Serve in shallow soup bowls garnished with dollops of fromage frais and dill fronds.

With Zest

A zester is one of the most useful little kitchen tools you can own. It has a plastic or wooden handle and a stainless steel blade with five tiny holes across the top. Scrape the blade across the surface of an unpeeled orange, lemon, or lime, and it will grate the aromatic zest into small slivers, leaving the bitter pith behind. Usually I like to zest the citrus fruit right over the saucepan or bowl so that the zest goes in, and some of the fragrant oils as well. (The oils add a lovely dimension of flavour, but the actual 'oiliness' is minuscule – it will not interfere with your low-fat regime.)

 VEGETABLE SOUP

Makes 5½ pts/3300 ml

This recipe is purposely designed to make a large quantity of soup. It really doesn't pay to embark on the chore of slicing, dicing, peeling, washing, etc., for a measly amount. Make it and freeze it in small containers. What luxury, at the end of a long, exhausting, aggravating day, to be able to conjure a feast like this from the freezer.

---

10 oz/300 g fresh spinach	3 inch/8 cm piece orange zest
2 large onions, cut in half and sliced into thin half-moons	1 bay leaf
3 cloves garlic, crushed	½ teaspoon dried oregano, crumbled
3 pts/1800 ml stock	½ teaspoon dried basil, crumbled
3 large carrots, peeled and thickly sliced	4 fl oz/120 ml tiny pasta
1 white turnip, peeled and diced	1 tin (14 oz/420 g) black-eyed beans, drained and rinsed
½ small swede, peeled and diced	Salt and freshly ground pepper to taste
1 large tin (1 lb 12 oz/840 g) plum tomatoes, undrained and crushed with the hands	4 oz/120 g frozen runner beans, thawed and thickly sliced
4 fl oz/120 ml dry red wine	4 fl oz/120 ml chopped parsley

---

1   Wash the spinach well. Strip the leaves off the stems. Shred the leaves. Reserve the stems.
2   Combine the onions, garlic and 8 fl oz/240 ml stock in a large pot that can be covered. Cover and boil for 5–7 minutes. Uncover, and simmer briskly until the onions are tender and beginning to stick to the pan, and the stock is almost gone. Splash in a bit more stock. Stir and scrape the browned bits on the bottom of the pan. When the onions are browned and

syrupy, stir in the carrots, turnip and swede. Stir and cook over a low heat for 2–3 minutes.

3   Stir in the tomatoes and their juices, the wine, the remaining stock, the orange peel, bay leaf, oregano and basil. Bring to the boil, partially cover and reduce heat. Simmer for 1–1½ hours until the vegetables are tender. Skim off scum occasionally.

4   Stir in the spinach stems, pasta, black-eyed beans, salt and pepper and runner beans. Simmer for 5–10 minutes more until the pasta is cooked.

5   Stir in the parsley and spinach leaves. Season to taste.

Note: The soup may be prepared in advance up through step 4. To serve, slowly bring to the boil. Stir in the parsley and spinach leaves. If you plan to freeze the soup, prepare it right through to step 5. Cool, then freeze in small containers.

Omit the black-eyed beans and the pasta. Substitute diced all-purpose potato.

GOULASH SOUP

Makes 3½ pts/2100 ml

I discovered Hungarian food the week of my honeymoon, almost thirty years ago, and I've been fascinated by the subtle and complex cuisine ever since. In 1972 I prepared a Hungarian dinner party for a group of influential people, and as a result (one influential person wrote to her editor about me) I was invited to write my first cook book. So you might say that Hungarian gastronomy looms large in my life. The Hungarians have a predilection for lard, cream and sour cream; converting this richness to Slim Cuisine without losing the underlying splendid Hungarian character has been a labour of love. This version of the great Hungarian classic is based on the quintessential bowl of goulash soup, experienced on a recent trip to Hungary, at a farm in the countryside near Budapest. The cook (brilliant man) enriched his soup with quantities of whole garlic cloves. The result is *sweet* and luscious, *not strong*! I'd like to write it in neon letters across the sky. Don't be afraid! The soup has a gentle and subtle character and will comfort and sustain you – it will not smite you with vulgarity.

51

2 Spanish onions, peeled and coarsely chopped	1 lb/480 g well-trimmed rump skirt steak, cut into 1 inch/2.5 cm cubes
10 fl oz/300 ml stock	
2 tablespoons hot paprika or paprika paste (or use half hot, half sweet)	4 pts/2400 ml stock
	Salt to taste
½ tablespoon lightly crushed caraway seeds	1 lb/480 g all-purpose potatoes, peeled and diced into 1 inch/2.5 cm cubes
Peeled whole cloves from 1 head garlic	

1   Combine onions and stock in a heavy flameproof casserole that can be covered. Cover and bring to the boil. Boil for 3–5 minutes. Uncover and simmer until it is almost dry and the onions are starting to brown.

2   Remove from heat. Add paprika and caraway. Stir for a moment or two. Stir in the garlic and the beef.

3   Add stock and a bit of salt. Cover and simmer for 1½–2 hours, until the meat is almost tender. Remove from heat, cool and then refrigerate overnight.

4   Next day, scrape off and discard congealed fat. Bring the soup to a boil. Reduce heat, add potatoes and a bit more salt if needed, and simmer, covered, for 20–30 minutes, until the meat and potatoes are tender.

'What do you think? Young women of rank actually eat – you will never guess what – garlick! Our poor friend Lord Byron is quite corrupted by living among these people.'

Percy Bysshe Shelley, in a letter from Naples

♡ ❄ ROOT VEGETABLE SOUP

Makes 2¾ pts/1650 ml

Root vegetables, mellow sweet garlic, fennel, and a mustard, wine, soy sauce flavour base, combine to make a deeply satisfying, hearty soup. It is almost a stew, and would make a delicious winter main dish, accompanied by a loaf of crusty wholemeal bread.

1 head garlic, each clove peeled but left whole	2 pts/1200 ml stock
	½ teaspoon dried tarragon, crumbled
1 Spanish onion, peeled, cut in half, then into ½ inch/1.25 cm wedges	1 tablespoon Dijon mustard
1 bulb fennel, trimmed and cut into ½ inch/1.25 cm wedges	2 tablespoons tomato paste
	3–4 dashes soy sauce

1 small swede, peeled and cut into
    ½ inch/1.25 cm pieces
1 large parsnip, peeled and cut
    into ½ inch/1.25 cm pieces
2 carrots, peeled and sliced into
    ½ inch/1.25 cm slices
2 stalks celery, sliced into
    ½ inch/1.25 cm pieces

4 fl oz/120 ml red wine
Juice of ½ large lemon
Salt and freshly ground pepper to
    taste
1 piece Parmesan rind
1 tin (14 oz/420 g) white beans,
    drained and rinsed

---

1   Put vegetables into a large, heavy, non-reactive pot with
    4 fl oz/120 ml stock. Cover and simmer for approximately
    5 minutes. Uncover and simmer for 5 minutes more, stirring
    occasionally.
2   Pour in the remaining stock. Stir together remaining in-
    gredients except the Parmesan rind and the beans. Add the
    mixture to the soup. Add the Parmesan rind. Season to taste.
3   Simmer, partially covered, for 40 minutes.
4   Stir in the beans. Taste and adjust seasoning. Simmer for
    10–15 minutes more, until the ingredients are very tender.

   Omit the white beans.

'One day I did not sing at all. The major sent for me.
    "Why do you not sing today, Caruso?"
    "I cannot sing on greasy soup."
Next day my soup was strong and there was no grease on it.'

            Enrico Caruso, in a newspaper interview

BLACK BEAN SOUP

Makes 3½ pts/2100 ml

A velvety purply-brown purée made from the noble black bean,
the best – in my opinion – of all the dried pulses. It's worth
searching for the beans (sometimes called turtle beans) in health
food and wholefood stores.

2½ pts/1500 ml soaked and cooked
    Black Beans (page 96)
2 pts/1200 ml stock
Grated zest of 1 small orange
¼ pt/150 ml dry sherry
Juice of 1 small orange

Steamed or boiled white rice
    (optional)
Fromage frais
A thinly sliced, peeled orange
Coriander leaves

---

1   Combine beans, stock and orange zest in a saucepan. Simmer
     for 15 minutes. Cool.
2   In batches, purée the soup in a liquidizer. (Fill the container
     less than half full for each batch.) Then rub the purée through a
     sieve. Return to the saucepan.
3   Pour in the sherry and orange juice. Simmer for 10 minutes.
     Taste and adjust seasonings.
4   If you are using the rice, put a spoonful in the bottom of a
     warm soup bowl. Fill with soup. Put a dollop of fromage frais
     on the surface, and lay two orange slices on each side of the
     dollop. Sprinkle with coriander leaves and serve at once.

'Soups feed you
Beans for vitamins . . .
Soups that nourish
Make hope flourish
Beans for nutrition
Beans for ambition
The Best People are crazy about soups!
Beans are all the rage among the Higher Income Groups!'

From the opera *Paul Bunyan*, libretto:
W. H. Auden, score: Benjamin Britten

 FISH SOUP

Makes 2½ pts/1500 ml

Excellent quality stock is essential to the success of this recipe. The
soup has a delicate and haunting quality. Make it a main dish soup
by adding 1 lb/480 g plaice fillets and 1 lb/450 g cod fillets (both of
them skinned and cut into 1 inch/2.5 cm cubes) in step 6. Stir for 3–5
minutes until cooked through. Sprinkle with chopped parsley.

---

2 large heads garlic	*1 pt/600 ml chicken stock*
2 large baking potatoes	*Cayenne pepper*
Juice of ½–1 small lemon	*Salt and freshly ground pepper*
Salt to taste	*Toasted French bread, sliced*
4–5 tablespoons fromage frais	*Raw garlic cloves*
1 pt/600 ml fish stock	

---

1   Preheat oven to 400° F, 200° C, Gas Mark 6.
2   Wrap garlic heads in a sheet of foil, shiny side in. Wash
     potatoes, dry and pierce in several places with a thin skewer or

fork. Bake both garlic and potatoes for 1–1½ hours until tender.

3   Scoop the potato flesh out of the skins (save the skins for another use, see page 43 or 109). Mash with a potato masher.

4   Squeeze the softened garlic into the potatoes. With an electric beater, beat the garlic and potatoes into a creamy mass. Beat in lemon juice and salt to taste and the fromage frais. Set aside in a non-reactive bowl.

5   Combine the stocks in a non-reactive pot. Bring to the boil. Boil for 3–5 minutes.

6   Ladle out ¾ pt/450 ml of stock. With a wire whisk, whisk the hot liquid into the potato-garlic mixture. Stir the mixture back into the soup. Stir over low heat until thoroughly amalgamated and hot. Add a pinch of cayenne pepper, salt and freshly ground pepper to taste. Serve at once with toasted French bread slices that have been rubbed with raw garlic cloves.

 Use the microwave for steps 1 and 2 (see pages 17 and 108).

GAZPACHO

Makes 3 pts/1800 ml

This is a variation on Gazpacho, not at all the classic version. You will find it refreshing, herby and very beautiful, especially served in clear glass bowls.

---

2 tins (1 lb 12 oz/840 g each) Italian tomatoes	2 cloves garlic, minced
4 fresh ripe tomatoes, peeled and seeded	2 tablespoons chopped fresh parsley
	2 tablespoons chopped fresh mint
Finely chopped fresh chilli peppers to taste, or chopped tinned chillies, or a mixture	4 red peppers, or 2 red peppers and 2 yellow peppers, grilled (see page 24) and coarsely chopped
2 fl oz/60 ml red wine vinegar	

---

1   Drain the tinned tomatoes (save the juice). Chop the tinned and fresh tomatoes.

2   Combine all ingredients, including tomato juice, in a non-reactive bowl. Chill thoroughly.

 Use tinned tomatoes only, and use tinned peppers.

❄ BEETROOT BORSCHT

Makes 4½ pts/2700 ml

Traditionally beetroot borscht is served cold, sometimes with a steaming hot potato nestled in the centre of each icy bowlful.

10 large beetroots, peeled and coarsely grated	*3½ pts/2100 ml water*
	2 fl oz/60 ml tomato paste
4 ripe tomatoes, peeled, seeded and chopped	*4 fl oz/120 ml lemon juice*
	1½ oz/45 g sugar
3 leeks, cleaned, trimmed and chopped (see note)	*Salt to taste*
	Fromage frais

1   Combine beets, tomatoes, leeks and water in a heavy pot that can be covered. Bring to the boil, reduce heat and simmer for 1 hour, partially covered.
2   Add tomato paste, lemon juice, sugar and salt. Simmer for an additional 30 minutes. Remove from heat.
3   Taste carefully and add additional lemon juice, sugar, or salt if necessary. The soup should be tart, but not unpleasantly so.
4   Cool, and then chill. Serve with a dollop of fromage frais on top of each serving.

Note: To trim leeks, cut off tip and 'beard'. Cut off and discard most of green portion, leaving just 1 inch/2.5 cm of green. With a sharp knife, slash through part of the white bulb and up through the remaining green portion. Wash leeks well under cold running water, holding them apart at the slash to wash away sand. Then chop and proceed with the recipe.

 Substitute low-Calorie sweetener for the sugar. Add it after the soup has cooled.

Main Dishes

'Cooking is like love. It should be entered into with
abandon, or not at all.'

Harriet van Horne

Fish

♡ ❄ ## CALIFORNIA-STYLE CIOPPINO

Makes 5½ pts/3300 ml

A full-fledged cioppino would contain lobster and clams in addition to the fish and shellfish listed here, but this slightly abbreviated version is just as delectable. The dish may be prepared with fish fillets only, if you can't find, or don't want, the prawns and mussels.

---

2 large Spanish onions, chopped
Approximately 1 pt/600 ml chicken stock, fish stock, or a combination
1 green or yellow pepper, seeded, peeled and chopped
2 cloves garlic, crushed
2 tins (14 oz/420 g each) chopped tomatoes
2 tablespoons tomato paste
12 fl oz/360 ml dry white wine
Salt and freshly ground pepper to taste

4 lb/1.92 kg firm white fish fillets (use a combination; choose from cod, halibut, haddock, sole, etc.) skinned and cut into 1 inch/2.5 cm cubes
1 lb/480 g medium-sized prawns, shelled and de-veined
16–18 large fresh mussels, thoroughly scrubbed and de-bearded
4 fl oz/120 ml chopped fresh parsley
Croûtons (see below)
Red Pepper and Garlic Spread (see page 45)

---

1   Combine onions and 10 fl oz/300 ml stock in a large, heavy, non-reactive flameproof casserole that can be covered. Cover and bring to the boil. Boil for 5 minutes. Uncover, stir in pepper and garlic, and boil until the stock is almost gone and the onions are beginning to brown.

2   Add the tomatoes, tomato paste, wine, 12 fl oz/360 ml stock, salt and pepper to taste. Simmer, partially covered, for 25 minutes.
3   Uncover and add the fish. Cover tightly and simmer very gently for 3 minutes.
4   Uncover and add the prawns, mussels and parsley. Cover tightly and simmer gently for 3–5 minutes more, or until the mussels open. Discard any mussels that do not open. Sprinkle with parsley. Serve from the casserole. Pass Croûtons spread with the Red Pepper and Garlic Spread.

Croûtons
Slice a French baguette. Bake the slices on the oven rack at 300° F, 150° C, Gas Mark 2, until dried through but not browned.

Note: Leftovers reheat very successfully in the microwave.

(🕐)   Omit mussels – they seem to take forever to clean!

♡ 🕐   **SMOKY FISH CHOWDER**

Makes 4 pts/2400 ml

Serve as a main dish, with a big mixed green salad dressed with balsamic vinegar and plenty of crusty bread.

1 large onion, coarsely chopped	*1 lb/480 g smoked haddock,*
1⅕ pts/720 ml fish stock	*skinned, boned and cut into*
2 fl oz/60 ml dry white wine	*1 inch/2.5 cm cubes (use*
1 pt/600 ml skimmed milk	*smoked haddock that has not*
3 medium all-purpose potatoes,	*been dyed)*
steamed until almost tender,	*6 oz/180 g peeled, cooked, tiny*
peeled and coarsely diced	*prawns*
1 lb/480 g firm white fish fillets,	*Freshly ground pepper to taste*
skinned and cut into	*Freshly chopped parsley*
1 inch/2.5 cm cubes	

1   Combine onion, ⅕ pt/120 ml stock and wine in a heavy-bottomed large pan. Cover and bring to the boil. Boil for 5 minutes. Uncover and boil until the onions are meltingly tender and beginning to brown.
2   Stir in remaining stock and milk. Bring to a simmer. Add potatoes and simmer gently for 3–5 minutes.
3   Stir in fish cubes. Barely simmer for 2–3 minutes. Stir in prawns and let heat through. Season with pepper and serve at once, sprinkled with fresh parsley.

'Chowder for breakfast, and chowder for dinner, and chowder for supper, 'till you begin to look for fish-bones coming through your clothes.'

Herman Melville, *Moby Dick*

♡ ⏰ **SOLE WITH VERMOUTH**

Makes 6 pieces

This is an exquisite dinner party dish. The preparation couldn't be easier. Use the freshest fish possible (never frozen fillets).

6 fillets of sole	Juice of 1 small lemon
Salt and freshly ground pepper to taste	¼ teaspoon dried thyme or 1 teaspoon chopped fresh thyme
4 fl oz/120 ml dry vermouth	4 fl oz/120 ml sliced spring onions
4 fl oz/120 ml Fish Stock (see page 14)	4 fl oz/120 ml chopped fresh parsley

1   Preheat oven to 400° F, 200° C, Gas Mark 6.
2   Trim fillets (freeze the trimmings for a future fish stock). Place fillets, skin side down, in one layer, in a shallow baking dish. Sprinkle with salt and pepper.
3   In a small non-reactive saucepan, combine vermouth, stock, lemon juice and thyme. Boil down until reduced by half. Pour over fish. Scatter on the spring onions and parsley.
4   Bake uncovered for 7–10 minutes, until opaque and cooked through. Serve at once, with rice, Wheat Pilaf (page 134), or steamed new potatoes.

⏰ **STEAMED FISH BUNDLE**

Serves 1

An absolutely beautiful dish with its heaps of brilliantly coloured, lightly cooked vegetables surrounding the pearly, smoky fish. It was inspired by a dish sampled at one of my old haunts, the scintillating Legal Seafood in Cambridge, Massachusetts. This makes enough for one; prepare as many bundles as you wish. After 20 minutes, unwrap one bundle to check if the fish is done. (If it is, it will fall into moist flakes at the touch of a fork.) A piece of *fresh* haddock fillet, or even cod, may be substituted for the smoked haddock (don't use the kind of smoked haddock that has been dyed). If using *fresh* fillets, sprinkle with a tiny bit of salt before wrapping.

1 piece (4–5 oz/120–150 g) smoked
   haddock fillet
1 small carrot, peeled and cut into
   thin sticks approximately 2
   inches/5 cm long and ¼ inch/0.6
   cm thick
1 small courgette, thinly sliced
½ red, ½ yellow pepper, peeled and
   cut into 2 inch/5 cm squares
2–3 fresh shiitake mushrooms,
   trimmed of the stems and
   quartered
2–3 small oyster or cultivated
   mushrooms, quartered
6 cherry tomatoes, halved
1 tablespoon chopped parsley
1 tablespoon sliced spring onion
1½ tablespoons fish, chicken, or
   vegetable stock
1½ tablespoons dry vermouth
1 level tablespoon grated Parmesan
   cheese
Freshly ground pepper

1   Preheat oven to 450° F, 230° C, Gas Mark 8.
2   Overlap two sheets of 12 × 16 inch/30 × 41 cm aluminium foil
    to form a 12 × 19 inch/30 × 48 cm rectangle. Put the fish, skin
    side down, in the centre. Arrange the carrots, courgettes,
    peppers and mushrooms around the fish in separate piles.
    Place the cherry tomatoes, cut sides up, on the fish. Sprinkle
    on the parsley and green onion. Dribble on the stock and
    vermouth. Sprinkle with cheese. Grind on some black pepper.
    Fold the flaps of foil over and seal the top and edges to form a
    well-sealed, loose tent around the fish and vegetables.
3   Bake packet on the oven shelf for 20–25 minutes. When done,
    slash the foil along the bottom and slide fish and vegetables on
    to a warm plate.

♡ Omit cheese.

♡   **ASPARAGUS WITH PRAWN
                    SAUCE**

Serves 4

Asparagus and prawns go together like Ginger and Fred. This
makes a stunning first course for a gala dinner, or a springtime
main dish. For a main dish, you may want to increase the amount
of asparagus. (As far as I'm concerned, no matter how much
asparagus there is, it's never enough.)

2 lb/960 g thick asparagus
1 lb/480 g tiny shelled prawns
Chopped fresh parsley
1 recipe 'Russian' Dressing
   (see page 62)

61

1   Cut off the tough woody stems of the asparagus stalks. With a swivel-bladed peeler, peel the stalks from the stem up to the buds. Wash well under cold running water. Steam over boiling water until 'crisp-tender' (a stalk should bend just a little, when held up with tongs), 3–6 minutes. Rinse under cold water to stop cooking, drain and set aside until needed.
2   Spread the asparagus out on a plate. Fold together 'Russian' Dressing and prawns. Spoon the prawns and sauce over the asparagus stems. Sprinkle with parsley.

'Russian' Dressing

Makes approximately 6 fl oz/180 ml

This is based on an old-fashioned, very fattening American classic. The original contains mayonnaise; this version contains those invaluable Slim Cuisine staples, buttermilk and fromage frais. Use as a salad dressing or a sauce for cold peeled prawns.

---

3 fl oz/90 ml buttermilk
3 tablespoons fromage frais
1½ tablespoons tomato paste
1 tablespoon minced spring onions
1 tablespoon drained chopped capers
*   (optional)*
1 tablespoon minced parsley

1 teaspoon grainy mustard – use
*   New York Deli Mustard if*
*   available (page 138)*
¼ teaspoon Worcestershire sauce
¼ teaspoon sugar – if you haven't
*   used New York Deli Mustard*

Whisk all ingredients together.

⊕   Use thin asparagus – they do not need to be peeled.

Meat

'To be put into the grave without ever enjoying a mouthful
of good meat is inhuman.'

Bertolt Brecht, trans. Lee Baxendell,
To Eat of Meat Joyously

CHINESE BEEF WITH ONIONS

Makes 1½ pts/900 ml

Switching to Slim Cuisine means ditching sesame oil, peanut oil
and all the other oily essentials of Chinese cuisine. I was delighted
to discover that stir-'frying' in stock can produce a very Chinese-
tasting dish. As with most Chinese cookery, have everything
diced, measured, sliced, crushed, etc., and laid out in logical order
on your work surface. At the last minute, stir-fry furiously and
serve at once.

1 goose skirt steak (about 1¼ lb/600 g), well trimmed	Approximately 8 fl oz/240 ml stock
2 tablespoons teriyaki sauce	1 large Spanish onion, cut in half and sliced into half-moons
2 tablespoons dry sherry	2 cloves garlic, crushed
1 tablespoon cornflour	Chopped fresh parsley and coriander for garnish
2 thin slices peeled ginger root, minced	

1   With a very sharp carving knife, slice the steak on the diagonal, against the grain, into slices that are as thin as you

63

can manage. Whisk together the teriyaki sauce, sherry and cornflour until the cornflour is dissolved. In a large bowl, with two spoons, toss the cornflour mixture with the beef, until the strips are well coated. Cover and set aside at room temperature for an hour.

2   Heat a large non-stick wok or frying pan. Pour in 2 fl oz/60 ml stock. When it boils furiously, dump in the meat. With two wooden paddles, constantly toss and turn the meat. Use the paddles to pull apart the strips as they cook. When they have lost their red raw look (about 2 minutes) scoop on to a plate. Cover loosely with foil and set aside.

3   Immediately pour 4 fl oz/120 ml of stock into the wok along with the onions and garlic. Stir once, cover and cook over high heat for 5 minutes. Uncover. Stir and cook over high heat until the onions are tender and surrounded by a scant, thick sauce.

4   Return the beef to the wok along with the meat juices that have accumulated. Season with a bit of salt if necessary. Stir together to mingle and heat through, about 1 minute. Heap on to a plate and sprinkle with herbs. Serve at once, with steamed rice or Wheat Pilaf (page 134), Savoury Peppers (page 124) and Spicy Sprouts (page 128).

CHINESE BEEF WITH MUSHROOMS

Makes 1½ pts/900 ml

This is a variation on the previous recipe, with the added allure of the intense smoky taste of reconstituted dried Chinese mushrooms. The mushrooms are available in Chinese groceries and some supermarkets and delicatessen.

1 oz/30 g dried Chinese mushrooms	¼ lb/120 g button mushrooms,
1 pt/600 ml warm water	quartered
1 goose skirt steak (about	1 bunch (about 10) thin spring
1¼ lb/600 g)	onions, trimmed and cut into
2 tablespoons teriyaki sauce	1½ inch/4 cm pieces
2 tablespoons dry sherry	Chopped fresh parsley and
1 tablespoon cornflour	coriander for garnish
Approximately 8 fl oz/240 ml stock	

1   Place the dried mushrooms in a bowl. Pour on the warm water and let them soak for ½–1 hour. Drain through a coffee filter, reserving the liquid. Rinse the mushrooms under cold running water. Squeeze dry. Trim off and discard the stems, and cut each mushroom in half.

2   With a very sharp carving knife, slice the steak on the diagonal, against the grain, into slices that are as thin as you can manage. Whisk together the teriyaki sauce, sherry and cornflour until the cornflour is dissolved. In a large bowl, with two wooden spoons, toss the cornflour mixture with the beef, until the strips are well coated. Cover and set aside at room temperature for 1 hour.

3   Heat a large non-stick wok or frying pan. Pour in 2 fl oz/60 ml stock. When it boils furiously, dump in the meat. With two wooden paddles constantly toss and turn the meat. Use the paddles to pull apart the strips as they cook. When they have lost their red raw look (about 2 minutes) scoop on to a plate. Cover loosely with foil and set aside.

4   Immediately pour 2 fl oz/60 ml stock, 2 fl oz/60 ml of the mushroom liquid and 1 fl oz/30 ml sherry into the wok. Dump in the Chinese mushrooms and the button mushrooms. Stir and cook over high heat until the mushrooms are surrounded by a scant, thick sauce. Stir in the spring onions and cook for another 30–40 seconds.

5   Return the beef to the wok along with the meat juices that have accumulated. Season with a bit of salt if necessary. Stir together to mingle and heat through, about 1 minute. Heap on to a plate and sprinkle with herbs. Serve at once with rice or Wheat Pilaf (page 134).

PEPPERED STEAK WITH MUSHROOM SAUCE

Serves 6

Goose skirt cooked this way is a snap to prepare, and can be served up in less than 30 minutes. Have the onions and mushrooms cooking in separate frying pans, then cook the steak. If you are in the habit of keeping Slim Cuisine Sautéed Mushrooms and 'Fried' Onions in the freezer, the job gets even easier. Any leftovers make one of the best sandwiches you have ever eaten. (Spread the bread with New York Deli Mustard, page 138.)

---

1 goose skirt steak, approximately 1½ lb/720 g	2 tablespoons chopped parsley
Freshly ground pepper to taste	Pinch or two of crumbled dried tarragon
Salt to taste	1 garlic clove, crushed
6 fl oz/180 ml red wine	Sautéed Mushrooms (page 22)
3 spring onions, trimmed and thinly sliced	'Fried' Onions (page 23)

---

1   Grind pepper over both sides of the meat and press it in. Let stand for 15 minutes.
2   Heat a heavy non-stick frying pan until moderately hot. Sear the meat on both sides. Use tongs to turn the meat.
3   Reduce the heat a bit and cook for 3–4 minutes on each side, until it feels springy, not mushy, when poked with your finger. Salt lightly on both sides. Remove to a warm plate, cover loosely with foil and keep warm.
4   Pour wine into the hot frying pan. While it fumes and sizzles, scrape up the brown bits with a wooden spoon or spatula. Stir in onions, herbs and garlic. When reduced and syrupy, stir in the Sautéed Mushrooms and their juices.
5   Pour in any juices that have accumulated under the steak. Slice the steak, thinly, against the grain.
6   Put a bed of 'Fried' Onions on a plate. Overlap the steak slices on the onions. Top with the mushroom sauce.

Befriend Your Butcher

My sincere advice is to make friends with your butcher, although it can get out of hand. In Atlanta, Georgia, where I once lived, I looked a new butcher straight in the eye, smiled my sweetest smile, and asked a few earnest questions about beef brisket. Later, walking back to the car, there was the new butcher; he had flung off his apron and followed me to the car park. It was my fattest time, 15½ quivering stones (much too fat to squeeze my wedding ring on to my finger), and the butcher, riveted by my sincere gaze and thinking I was unattached and vastly beautiful, asked me out. Alas, it was a professional relationship I was after, to be conducted over the counter, involving learned exchanges about brisket, flank and tenderloin, resulting in the butcher tenderly wrapping choice cuts for my family's evening meal.

But still – it pays to court your butcher's good will. There are several cuts of beef not readily available at the supermarket that you should ask him to supply regularly for you.

1   **Goose skirt steak** (sometimes called flank skirt). A flat, *lean*, paddle-shaped, deeply flavoured cut of meat, perfect for grilling or pan frying.
2   **Rump skirt steak.** A fibrous, rich-in-gelatine cut, that makes excellent full-flavoured stews with copious juices.
3   **Brisket.** The butcher will have plenty of these, but for your purposes it must be cut as follows:

(a) boned;
(b) the point end separated from the smaller flank end and both pieces mercilessly trimmed of *every* scrap of fat. No matter how earnestly you explain this and how sincere your gaze, the butcher will not trim off enough fat. You will still need to do some additional trimming when you get home. The point end of the brisket makes a superb braised joint (see below) and the flank end is excellent cut into cubes and stewed.

GRILLED GOOSE SKIRT
STEAK

Serves 6

Goose skirt is the perfect cut of meat for outdoor grilling. On a charcoal grill it cooks in no time at all and feeds a lot of people happily on an economical amount of meat. One goose skirt (1½–2 lb/720–960 g) will feed six people or more, depending on the accompaniments. For a barbecue, marinate the steak (see marinade below). Depending on the intensity of flavour you want, marinate from 1 to 24 hours.

Line your hibachi or charcoal grill with foil, shiny side up. This makes cleaning up easier and reflects heat. Never use a chemical starter on the charcoal; it will impart a revolting flavour to the meat. Use spills made from rolled-up paper. Start your fire at least 30 minutes before cooking time, and do not begin to cook until you have a good bed of glowing coals covered with a bed of white ash, and *no* flames.

Use tongs to turn the meat on the grill; a fork would make holes that allow delicious juices to drip away. A goose skirt steak should be cooked rare (red inside) or medium rare (pink) or it will not be tender. Make sure the meat is at room temperature, then cook it 4–5 minutes on each side for rare, 5–6 for medium rare. To check for doneness, poke it in the centre with your finger. If it feels very *soft* and mushy it is very rare, almost raw in fact. The firmer it gets, the more done. When it feels firmish but springy it is medium rare. As the steak cooks, brush it with marinade. If you just like the taste of good meat, don't bother with marinade, simply cover the steak with a good coating of freshly ground peppercorns.

When the meat is done, let it rest for 3 minutes, then slice it thinly, with a sharp knife, diagonally against the grain. Serve it with *Slim Cuisine I*'s Browned Onions and New York Deli Mustard (page 138).

Marinade for Goose Skirt

3 tablespoons soy sauce	Pinch sugar
4 tablespoons lemon juice	Salt and freshly ground pepper to taste
6 tablespoons tomato paste	3 tablespoons water

'Four rare steaks please and hurry. We haven't eaten in five hundred and seventy-six thousand million years.'

Douglas Adams, *The Restaurant at the End of the Universe*

❄ BRAISED BRISKET OF BEEF

Serves 6–8

Perfect for Sunday lunch. Make it ahead of time, and then devote yourself to the vegetables on the day. The gravy is spectacularly rich and deeply flavoured, and the meat is buttery tender. I'll wager that you have never tasted a joint of meat to rival this one for tenderness and flavour. See above for advice on buying and cooking brisket.

1 point cut brisket (about 4 lb/1.92 kg) trimmed of all fat	Approximately 4 fl oz/120 ml sun-dried tomatoes, chopped (optional)
8 fl oz/240 ml beef or chicken stock	Salt and freshly ground pepper to taste
2 large Spanish onions, halved and sliced into thin half-moons	4 large garlic cloves, peeled and left whole
4 fl oz/120 ml red wine	2 carrots, peeled and sliced
2 fl oz/60 ml brandy	1 stalk celery with leaves, sliced
2 fl oz/60 ml tomato paste	3 sprigs parsley

1   Preheat oven to 350° F, 180° C, Gas Mark 4.
2   In a large non-stick frying pan sear the brisket on both sides. When the meat is browned on both sides, put it on a plate and loosely cover it with foil.
3   Pour any fat drippings out of the frying pan and blot the pan with paper towels, but do not wipe off the browned bits. Pour 4 fl oz/120 ml stock into the frying pan. Add the onion. Cover and boil for 4–5 minutes. Uncover, turn down the heat and cook gently. When it is browned and almost tender, pour in the wine and brandy. Boil, scraping the pan with a wooden spoon to release all the browned bits. When the brandy has cooked away, stir in the tomato paste and optional sun-dried tomatoes. Season with a bit of salt and freshly ground pepper. Scrape the mixture into a 9 × 13 × 2 inch/23 × 33 × 5 cm baking pan. Pour the remaining stock over the onion.

4   Season the meat on both sides with salt and pepper. Place the meat on the onion. Pour in any meat juices that have accumulated on the plate. Tuck the garlic, carrot and celery slices, and parsley around the meat. Cover the baking pan tightly with heavy-duty aluminium foil, shiny side down.

5   Place the baking dish in the oven for 1 hour. Reduce the oven temperature to 250° F, 120° C, Gas Mark 1, and bake for an additional 2–2½ hours, or until very tender.

6   When tender, remove the meat to a plate and cover to prevent it drying out. Let cool. Discard the parsley and celery. Pour the pan juices and remaining vegetables into a jug, add any juices that have accumulated under the meat, cool and refrigerate. When the meat has cooled, wrap well in cling film and refrigerate.

7   On the next day, skim any fat from the juices in the jug. Purée the vegetables and juices in the liquidizer. Then rub the purée through a sieve.

8   With a sharp carving knife, slice the meat thinly against the grain and arrange in a baking dish. Pour and spread some of the puréed sauce over the slices. Cover and refrigerate until serving time. To serve, reheat, covered, for 35–40 minutes in the oven at 325° F, 160° C, Gas Mark 3. Reheat the remaining puréed sauce in a saucepan and serve in a gravy boat.

❋ BEEF CURRY

Makes 2½ pts/150 ml

The thick curry sauce that blankets the beef comes from an onion spice purée; it has a rich texture and deep taste, although it contains no fat. The method is very unconventional, but the result is very curry-like.

---

3 large onions, coarsely chopped
Approximately 1 pt/600 ml chicken
   stock
1 teaspoon fresh ginger root, peeled
   and minced
2 cloves garlic, minced
1 teaspoon each: ground cumin,
   ground coriander, ground
   turmeric, sweet paprika or
   paprika paste, mild chilli powder

¼–½ teaspoon ground cayenne
   pepper
3 lb/1.44 kg very well trimmed
   rump skirt, or flank end
   brisket (see page 66), cut into
   ¾ inch/2 cm cubes
1 tablespoon tomato paste
Salt and freshly ground pepper to
   taste
1 teaspoon garam masala

---

1   Preheat the oven to 350° F, 180° C, Gas Mark 4.

2   Separate the segments of the onion pieces and spread them in a heavy frying pan. (Do *not* use a non-stick pan.) Add *no* liquid

or fat. Heat the frying pan gently. Cook at moderate heat, without stirring, until the onions are sizzling and beginning to stick to the pan.

3   Stir in 10 fl oz/300 ml of stock and let it bubble up. Stir in the ginger, garlic and spices. Turn the heat down a bit and simmer, stirring frequently, until the mixture is very thick (not at all soupy), and the onions and spices are 'frying' in their own juices. Don't rush this step, it is essential that the spices should not have a raw harsh taste. Cook very gently for a few more minutes.

4   Scrape half of the onion-spice mixture into the container of the liquidizer. Purée. Pour the purée into a baking dish.

5   Stir in the unpuréed onion-spice mixture, the beef and tomato paste. Season to taste with salt and pepper.

6   Cover tightly and bake for 2–2½ hours until the meat is very tender. Adjust the oven temperature down during the cooking time to maintain a gentle simmer. It must not boil.

7   Dump the curry into a sieve or colander, over a large bowl. Put the meat into a bowl and cover well so that it does not dry out. Pour the juices into a glass jug. Chill overnight. The fat will rise to the surface and congeal. Discard every speck of fat.

8   Recombine meat and juices. Stir in garam masala. Simmer for 10–15 minutes. Serve with Basmati rice, Herb Sauce (use coriander, page 137), a selection of vegetables and Curried Roast Potatoes (*Slim Cuisine I*).

❄   # STUFATINO

Makes 2½ pts/1500 ml

Use a good wine (the alcohol cooks away) and you will have a rich, fragrant and satisfying Italian beef stew with quantities of gorgeous juices. I once served this to 180 ravenous obesity scientists at an obesity conference at Downing College in Cambridge. In their enthusiasm for this dish and other Slim Cuisine delicacies that my staff and I set on the buffet table, they almost devoured the casserole dishes and tablecloth as well. *No one* puts away prodigious quantities of food the way obesity scientists do.

2 onions, cut in half and sliced into thin half-moons	4 cloves garlic, peeled but left whole
12 fl oz/360 ml stock	½ teaspoon dried rosemary
3 lb/1.44 kg well-trimmed rump skirt, or flank end brisket (see page 66), cut into 1½ inch/4 cm cubes	½ teaspoon dried marjoram
	Salt and pepper to taste
	2 tablespoons tomato paste
	8 fl oz/240 ml Italian dry red wine

70

1   Preheat the oven to 300° F, 150° C, Gas Mark 2.
2   Combine onions and stock in an 8 inch/20 cm frying pan. Cover and bring to the boil. Boil for 5 minutes. Uncover. Reduce heat and simmer briskly until just about dry and beginning to stick a little bit.
3   Lower the heat. Toss and stir constantly with a wooden spoon until you smell a lovely, toasty, oniony aroma and the bottom of the pan is beginning to brown just a bit. Pour in a splash of dry wine or additional stock and turn the heat up again. Stir with the wooden spoon, scraping up all the browned bits.
4   Stir in beef, garlic, seasonings, tomato paste and wine. Add stock, if necessary, to just barely cover the contents of the pot. Cover tightly and cook in the oven for 2–3 hours until the meat is fork tender. Adjust the oven temperature down during this time so that the contents of the pot remain at a gentle simmer.
5   Dump the meat into a colander over a bowl. Pour the drained juices into a large jug. Put the meat into a bowl. Cover the meat and the jug and refrigerate overnight.
6   Next day, scrape off congealed fat from the juices in the jug. Recombine the meat and juices. Reheat gently and serve with pasta, Polenta (page 114), or Mashed Potatoes (page 108).

✳ # STEFADO OF BEEF

Makes 3–3½ pts/1800–2100 ml

Stefado of beef is the Greek entry into the beef stew sweepstakes. It has a beautiful balance of sweet and sour.

---

3 lb/1.44 kg well-trimmed rump skirt, or flank end brisket (page 66), cut into 1 inch/2.5 cm cubes
Approximately 3 tablespoons tomato paste
4 fl oz/120 ml freshly chopped parsley
Salt and pepper to taste
1 bay leaf

1 teaspoon oregano, crumbled
1 teaspoon ground cinnamon
1 teaspoon ground cumin
½ teaspoon sugar
4 fl oz/120 ml dry white wine
4 fl oz/120 ml red wine vinegar
24 tiny boiling onions, peeled
4 fl oz/120 ml additional freshly chopped parsley

---

1   Preheat oven to 300° F, 150° C, Gas Mark 2.
2   Combine all ingredients except additional parsley. Mix very well.
3   Place in a heavy pot that can be covered. Cover tightly and simmer for 2 hours or until the meat is very tender, and the onions have almost disintegrated. Adjust oven temperature

during cooking time so contents of pot remain at a simmer. Do
not let it boil.
4   When tender, cool and refrigerate. Next day, discard congealed fat and reheat gently. Serve in a deep dish, garnished
with parsley. Serve with rice, Wheat Pilaf (page 134), or Roast
Potatoes (page 132).

❄ BEEF GOULASH

Makes 4½ pts/2700 ml

This is my family's favourite beef dish. I always have it in the
freezer in individual servings. As you comfort yourself with this
soul-warming stew, mull over the fact that peppers (including
paprika), tomatoes and potatoes, those staples of Hungarian cookery, were gifts of the New World and did not hit Hungary until the
Turks invaded, which is not that long ago in historic terms. The
Magyars knew nothing about such ingredients.

5 large onions, peeled and coarsely chopped	*3 cloves garlic, minced*
12 fl oz/360 ml stock	*3 lb/1.44 kg well-trimmed rump skirt, or flank end brisket*
1½ tablespoons Hungarian paprika or Hungarian paprika paste	*(see page 66), cut into 1 inch/2.5 cm cubes*
2 large peppers (1 green, 1 yellow if possible), peeled and coarsely chopped	*Salt and freshly ground pepper to taste*
	3 heaped tablespoons tomato paste

1   Preheat oven to 350° F, 180° C, Gas Mark 4.
2   Combine onions and stock in a non-reactive flameproof
casserole that can be covered. Cover and bring to the boil. Boil
for 5 minutes. Uncover. Reduce heat and simmer briskly,
stirring occasionally, until almost dry and beginning to brown
a bit. Stir in paprika. Stir for a few seconds over *low* heat.
3   Add remaining ingredients, and stir well to combine. Place in
oven and simmer for 2–3 hours, until the meat is very tender,
in a savoury thick sauce. Cool and then refrigerate overnight.
The next day, skim off fat. Serve the goulash in shallow soup
plates. Serve Mashed Potatoes (page 108) or Roast Potatoes
(page 132) on the side.

⏱ PORK IN MUSTARD SAUCE

Makes 2½ pints/1500 ml

Pork tenderloin is one of the leanest cuts of meat of all. It cooks very
quickly and yields elegant results.

2 well-trimmed pork tenderloins (approximately 12 oz/360 g each)

Salt and freshly ground pepper to taste

2 large Spanish onions, cut into wedges (cut each peeled onion in sixteenths, then separate the petals)

4 fl oz/120 ml stock

2 fl oz/60 ml white wine

3 peppers (use both red and yellow), seeded, cut into strips approximately ½ inch/1.25 cm wide, 1½ inches/3.75 cm long, and peeled

2 cloves garlic, minced

2 rounded teaspoons grainy mustard

1 rounded teaspoon Dijon mustard

2½ tablespoons fromage frais

Pinch of cayenne pepper (optional)

1 tablespoon freshly chopped parsley

---

1   Slice the pork tenderloins slightly on the diagonal into ½ inch/1.25 cm thick medallions.

2   Heat a large heavy-bottomed frying pan. When very hot, place a single layer of pork slices in the pan (they should not touch each other). Grind on some pepper. Let the pork slices brown (1–2 minutes). Then turn with tongs, sprinkle with salt, and brown for another minute or so on the second side. Remove to a plate and repeat until all the slices have been browned.

3   When all the pork slices are reposing on the plate, dump the onions, stock and wine into the frying pan. Let the liquid bubble up while you stir and scrape up the browned bits with a wooden spoon. Cover and cook on high heat for 2–3 minutes. Uncover, and add the peppers and garlic. Stir. Cover and cook for 4–5 minutes until the onions are cooked but retain a slight crispiness.

4   Add the mustards and stir to thoroughly coat the vegetables. Stir in 2 tablespoons of fromage frais and heat through. Do not boil.

5   Add pork slices and any accumulated meat juices. Sprinkle in cayenne. Stir and cook until the pork is heated through. Do not let the sauce boil. Add the additional ½ tablespoon of fromage frais. Stir well for a moment or so. Stir in parsley. Serve at once.

POT ROAST LAMB

Serves 6–8

The pot roasting method of cooking a leg of lamb results in extremely tender meat, with the wonderful flavour of the marinade penetrating right to the bone.

4 cloves garlic, crushed
3 medium onions, finely chopped
4 fl oz/120 ml dry red wine
1 tin (14 oz/420 g) chopped
    tomatoes, sieved or liquidized
10–12 sun-dried tomatoes, coarsely
    chopped (optional)
Juice of 1 lemon
Grated zest of 1 lemon

1 teaspoon each of ground allspice,
    cinnamon, cumin
½ teaspoon caster sugar
1 teaspoon dried oregano, crumbled
Salt and pepper to taste
1 very well trimmed leg of lamb –
    approximately 4 lb/1920 g
    (weight after fat has been
    trimmed)

1   In a large, non-reactive vessel, combine all ingredients except salt and pepper and lamb. Add lamb and turn to coat with mixture. Cover. Refrigerate for up to two days. Before cooking, allow to return to room temperature.
2   Place lamb in a roasting pan. Season with salt and freshly ground pepper. Pour the sauce over and around the meat. Cover very tightly with foil so that no steam can escape.
3   Roast at 350° F, 180° C, Gas Mark 4, for 2 hours. After 1 hour, uncover and baste. Re-cover tightly.
4   Remove lamb to a plate, cover loosely with foil and allow to rest while de-greasing the sauce.
5   Pour pan juices into a glass measuring jug and put into the freezer for 10–15 minutes. Take out and skim off the fat. Reheat. Slice the lamb and serve with the pan juices. If desired, the pan juices may be puréed in a liquidizer or pushed through a sieve.

VEAL SHANKS WITH WILD MUSHROOMS

Serves 6

Dried cèpes and morels can be purchased in many speciality food stores or the gourmet department of some supermarkets, but feel free to substitute if necessary. I have successfully used a mixture of fresh cultivated mushrooms and dried Chinese or Japanese shiitake mushrooms, available from Oriental food stores and some supermarkets. Sliced veal shank is sold in many supermarkets under the name 'osso buco' (hollow bone). One of the best things about this homely, warming dish is the gorgeous rich, thick gravy. Just the thing for an accompanying mound of mashed potatoes.

1 oz/30 g dried cèpes/porcini
1 oz/30 g dried morels
6 slices very well trimmed
    veal shank, each about
    1½ inches/4 cm thick

12 fl oz/360 ml dry red wine
20 cloves garlic, peeled (optional)
½ lb/240 g fresh mushrooms,
    quartered
Dash of soy sauce

1   Rinse the dried mushrooms briefly under cold running water, then soak them in warm water, to cover generously, for ½–1 hour. Strain the water through a cheesecloth-lined sieve or a coffee filter and reserve. Rinse the mushrooms under cold running water, and trim off and discard any tough stems.

2   Dry the veal. With a small sharp knife and a spoon cut and dig out the marrow from the hollow centre bone. Discard it. Brown the veal over a medium heat in a heavy-bottomed frying pan until lightly browned on both sides. Transfer to a plate.

3   Add 8 fl oz/240 ml of the red wine and 8 fl oz/240 ml of the mushroom-soaking liquid to the frying pan. Bring to the boil and let boil for 2 minutes, scraping the bottom of the pan with a wooden spoon or spatula. Reduce heat.

4   Return the veal shanks to the frying pan. Scatter in the garlic cloves. Season with salt and pepper to taste. Let simmer, covered, for about 20 minutes.

5   Meanwhile, put the fresh mushrooms and 4 fl oz/120 ml of dry red wine, a dash or two of soy sauce and 4 fl oz/120 ml of the mushroom-soaking liquid into a non-reactive, non-stick heavy frying pan. Stir to combine everything very well.

6   Simmer, stirring occasionally. At first the mushrooms will release a good deal of extra liquid. Continue simmering, stirring occasionally until the liquid is almost gone. Let the mushrooms 'fry' gently in their own juices for a few moments. Do not let them scorch or stick. Stir in the soaked dried mushrooms.

7   When the veal shanks have cooked for 20 minutes, turn them over. Add enough of the mushroom-soaking liquid to barely cover the veal shanks and the sautéed mushrooms to the frying pan. Cover and let the meat simmer for another 1½ hours or until it is meltingly tender and falling off the bones, and the liquid has cooked down to a thick, rich sauce. Baste with the pan juices occasionally.

8   Remove the veal and mushrooms to a serving plate, cover tightly and keep warm. Skim the fat from the sauce. Reheat briefly, then pour over the veal.

9   Serve at once.

❄ SHEPHERD'S PIE

Serves 8

My favourite shepherd's pies deviate from the norm: indeed they often contain a rather eccentric assortment of ingredients. Here, sultanas and red lentils stretch out a small amount of lamb and make it absolutely irresistible.

1 large Spanish onion, chopped
4 fl oz/120 ml red wine
1 pt/600 ml stock
2 medium carrots, peeled and diced
1 yellow pepper, peeled and diced
½ teaspoon each dried tarragon and
  thyme
¼ teaspoon each ground allspice
  and cinnamon
Pinch or two of ground cayenne
3 tablespoons tomato paste
1 tablespoon sultanas soaked in
  2 fl oz/60 ml red wine
4 oz/120 g split red lentils, washed,
  drained and picked over

½ lb/240 g very lean minced lamb,
  sautéed, drained and blotted
Salt and freshly ground pepper to
  taste

Potatoes (makes about 2 pts/
  1200 ml mashed potatoes)
Well-seasoned mashed potatoes
  made from 2 lb/960 g potatoes,
  salt and pepper
Generous pinch allspice
Generous pinch cayenne pepper
4 fl oz/120 ml buttermilk
6 tablespoons Parmesan cheese

1   Spread the onion pieces in a large, heavy, non-reactive pan. Cook over high heat, without stirring, until they are sizzling and beginning to stick to the pan.
2   Pour in 4 fl oz/120 ml red wine. Boil, stirring and scraping up the browned bits in the pan, until the liquid is just about gone.
3   Add 3 fl oz/90 ml stock. Cover and boil for 5 minutes. Reduce heat. Stir in carrots and peppers. Pour in 2 fl oz/60 ml stock. Cover and simmer gently for 5–10 minutes, until the carrots are beginning to get tender.
4   Stir in the herbs, spices, tomato paste, sultanas and their wine, the lentils, the lamb and salt and pepper. Stir in 8 fl oz/240 ml stock. Cover and simmer for 20 minutes, uncovering to stir occasionally. If it gets too dry and threatens to stick, add a bit more stock.
5   After 20 minutes, uncover and cook for 5–10 minutes more until the lentils are tender and the mixture is very thick.
6   Spread the lamb/vegetable mixture in a gratin pan. Season the potatoes with the allspice and cayenne pepper and beat in the buttermilk. Spread the potatoes over the meat mixture. Sprinkle evenly with Parmesan cheese. At this point the pie may be covered tightly with cling film and refrigerated for up to two days. Bring to room temperature before proceeding.
7   Preheat oven to 375° F, 190° C, Gas Mark 5. Bake the pie uncovered for 45–55 minutes until browned, puffed and bubbly. Serve at once, or cool, wrap tightly and freeze for a later meal. Reheat, covered, from the frozen state, either in the oven or the microwave.

✳ CURRIED SHEPHERD'S PIE

Serves 8

This is my all-time favourite shepherd's pie. I've made it many times and served it to the great and the near-great. Don't be afraid of the long list of ingredients – you are, basically, making your own curry powder with the long list of spices. The meat-aubergine mixture is at once hot, sweet and sour, and the potatoes are creamy and mellow with the taste of baked garlic.

---

2 large Spanish onions, coarsely chopped
10 fl oz/300 ml of stock
1 teaspoon turmeric
1 teaspoon cumin
1 teaspoon pure chilli powder
1 teaspoon ground coriander
1 teaspoon ground cardamoms
¼ teaspoon ground ginger
¼ teaspoon ground mustard
¼ teaspoon ground cinnamon
Pinch ground cloves, allspice and nutmeg
Salt and freshly ground pepper to taste
3 cloves of garlic, minced
1½ lb/720 g lean minced lamb
Chopped pulp of 2 Baked Aubergines (page 21) approximately ¾ lb/360 g each

1 tin (14 oz/420 g) chopped tomatoes
5 fl oz/150 ml raisins
4 tablespoons mango chutney
1 tablespoon fresh lemon juice
1 tablespoon Worcestershire sauce
8 dried apricot halves, minced (use scissors)
1 tablespoon tomato paste
Mashed potatoes made with 7 large baking potatoes, salt, pepper and 8 fl oz/240 ml buttermilk (see page 108)
¼ teaspoon cayenne pepper
½ teaspoon garam masala
Purée from 1 head Baked Garlic (page 17)

---

1   Spread the onions out in a heavy frying pan. Add *no* liquid or fat. Heat the frying pan gently. Cook at a moderate heat, without stirring, until the onions are sizzling, and beginning to stick to the pan.

2   Stir in the stock and let it bubble up, stirring up the browned deposits in the pan as it bubbles. Stir in the spices and the garlic. Turn down the heat and simmer, stirring frequently, until the mixture is very thick (not at all soupy) and the onions and spices are 'frying' in their own juices. Don't rush this step; it is essential that the spices do not have a harsh, raw taste. Taste. Cook very gently for a few more minutes if necessary. Scrape the mixture into a bowl.

3   In the same frying pan, cook the minced lamb over medium heat. As it browns, break up any lumps with a wooden spoon. When it is thoroughly cooked, drain *very* well in a colander set

over a bowl. Discard the drained fat. Put the lamb and the onion mixture back into the frying pan.

4   Stir in the aubergine, tomatoes, raisins, chutney, lemon juice, Worcestershire sauce and apricots. Simmer for 30 minutes, stirring occasionally. Stir in the tomato paste and simmer for 5–10 minutes more, until thick. Taste and adjust seasonings. Spread the mixture into a gratin pan. Preheat oven to 375° F, 190° C, Gas Mark 5.

5   Season the potatoes with cayenne pepper, garam masala, Baked Garlic purée and salt and pepper. Taste and add more seasoning if needed. Spread the potatoes over the meat.

6   Bake for 40–50 minutes until brown and bubbling.

Alternative Topping

For a change, microwave or steam all-purpose unpeeled potatoes (about 5) until tender, but not falling apart. Slice ¼ inch/0.6 cm thick and overlap on the surface of the lamb mixture in the gratin pan. Pour over this custard topping:

---

5 egg whites
16 fl oz/480 ml skimmed milk
Salt and freshly ground pepper to taste

¼ teaspoon cayenne pepper
½ teaspoon garam masala

---

1   Preheat oven to 325° F, 170° C, Gas Mark 3.

2   Beat together the eggs, milk and seasonings. Pour evenly over the potatoes. Bake for 50–60 minutes, until browned and set.

❋   # SWEET AND SOUR STUFFED CABBAGE

Makes approximately 20 cabbage rolls

Stuffed cabbage is always festive and heartwarming. Freezing the cabbage first, then thawing it when needed, makes the cabbage very easy to separate into individual leaves, and makes the leaves flexible enough to wrap around the stuffing easily. The stuffing and the sauce may be made a day or two in advance. Once wrapped and in the oven, the cabbage rolls bake for 2 hours, but totally unattended. As they bake, they fill the house with the happiest of smells. Make the stuffed cabbage ahead of time and refrigerate or freeze until needed. If you wish to cut the 2-hour baking time short, steam the unstuffed cabbage leaves for about 3 minutes at the end of step 1. Then the stuffed rolls need to be baked for only about 1 hour. But, personally, I'd rather have the ease of stuffing the leaves without the extra fiddling about of steaming.

1 large head frozen cabbage, thawed   *Stuffing (see below)*
  (see note above)   *Tomato-Pepper Sauce (see page 80)*

1   Separate the cabbage into individual leaves. Place each leaf, curved side up, on your work surface. With a sharp paring knife, pare down the tough vein. Turn each leaf curved side down.
2   Fill each leaf with a tablespoon or so of stuffing. Fold the end over the stuffing, fold in the sides and roll into a neat parcel. Place each filled parcel in a baking dish, seam-side down. They should fill the dish in one layer.
3   Spread the sauce evenly over the cabbage rolls and let it run down the sides. The dish may be refrigerated at this point for a day or two, or frozen.
4   Preheat oven to 350° F, 180° C, Gas Mark 4. Bake the cabbage, tightly covered, for 2 hours. Serve piping hot.

Stuffing

Makes 1½ pts/900 ml

1 large Spanish onion, chopped
4 fl oz/120 ml red wine
1 pt/600 ml stock
1 yellow pepper, peeled and diced
½ teaspoon each dried tarragon,
  thyme and cinnamon
¼ teaspoon ground allspice
Pinch or two of ground cayenne

3 tablespoons tomato paste
3 tablespoons sultanas soaked in
  2 fl oz/60 ml red wine
4 oz/120 g split red lentils, washed,
  drained and picked over
½ lb/240 g very lean minced lamb,
  sautéed, drained and blotted
Salt and freshly ground pepper to taste

1   Spread the onion pieces in a large, heavy, non-reactive pan. Cook over high heat, without stirring, until they are sizzling and beginning to stick to the pan.
2   Pour in 4 fl oz/120 ml red wine. Boil, stirring and scraping up the browned bits in the pan, until the liquid is just about gone.
3   Add 3 fl oz/90 ml stock. Cover and boil for 5 minutes. Reduce heat. Stir in pepper. Pour in 2 fl oz/60 ml stock. Cover and simmer gently for 5–10 minutes.
4   Stir in the herbs, spices, tomato paste, sultanas and their wine, the lentils, the lamb and salt and pepper. Stir in 8 fl oz/240 ml stock. Cover and simmer for 20 minutes, uncovering to stir occasionally. If it gets too dry and threatens to stick, add a bit more stock.
5   After 20 minutes, uncover and cook for 5–10 minutes more until the lentils are tender and the mixture is very thick.

Tomato-Pepper Sauce

Makes 2½ pts/1500 ml

---

2 red, 2 yellow peppers, grilled,
  peeled and coarsely chopped
  (substitute tinned red peppers if
  you are in a hurry)
12 ripe tomatoes, peeled, seeded,
  juiced and coarsely chopped
  (omit fresh tomatoes and
  increase the tinned tomatoes if
  you are in a hurry)
4 tins (14 oz/420 g each) chopped
  tomatoes
4 cloves garlic, minced

Salt and pepper to taste
Pinch of cayenne pepper
¼ teaspoon ground cumin
1 chilli pepper, minced (optional)
1½ tablespoons chopped fresh
  thyme
4 heaped tablespoons chopped
  parsley
1 tablespoon chopped fresh mint or
  basil
1 teaspoon fresh lemon or lime juice
½ teaspoon brown sugar

---

1   Combine all ingredients except herbs, citrus juice and sugar in a frying pan. Simmer uncovered for 30 minutes, until thickened.
2   Stir in fresh herbs, citrus juice and sugar. Simmer for 5 minutes more. Taste and adjust salt, pepper, sugar and citrus juice if necessary. It should have a good balance of sweet and sour.

Note: To prepare cabbage for stuffing, cut out the core several days in advance. Wrap the cored cabbage in clingfilm. Freeze. Thaw when needed.

'"Cool mountain water – and a stuffed cabbage. That's all I eat."
  "Is stuffed cabbage allowed on your diet?"
  "Who the hell cares if it's allowed! I love it!"'

Mel Brooks, *The 2013 Year Old Man*

   # STUFFED PEPPERS

Makes 18 pieces

This was inspired by a beautiful dish of stuffed peppers served at Justin DeBlank's restaurant in London's Duke Street.

---

9 red peppers, cut in half (discard
  seeds and ribs) and peeled (use
  a swivel-bladed peeler, the
  microwave, or the grill – see
  page 24)
1 large Spanish onion, coarsely
  chopped

¼ teaspoon ground allspice
Pinch or two of cayenne pepper
3 tablespoons tomato paste
3 tablespoons sultanas soaked in
  2 fl oz/60 ml red wine
½ lb/240 g very lean minced beef,
  sautéed, drained and blotted

---

4 fl oz/120 ml dry red wine	4 oz/120 g bulghur (cracked wheat),
5 fl oz/150 ml stock	soaked for 30 minutes in water
2 medium carrots, peeled and diced	to cover and squeezed dry
1 yellow pepper, peeled and diced	Salt and freshly ground pepper to
½ teaspoon each dried tarragon,	taste
dried thyme, ground cinnamon	Yoghurt Herb Sauce (see below)

1   Arrange peppers, cut sides up, in a shallow baking dish.

2   Spread onion pieces in a large, heavy, non-reactive frying pan. Cook over high heat, without stirring, for a minute or two, until they are sizzling and beginning to stick to the pan.

3   Pour in 4 fl oz/120 ml of red wine. Boil, stirring and scraping up the browned bits in the pan, until the liquid is just about gone.

4   Add 3 fl oz/90 ml of stock. Cover and boil for 5 minutes. Reduce heat.

5   Stir in carrots and yellow peppers. Pour in 2 fl oz/60 ml of stock. Cover and simmer gently for 5–10 minutes, until the carrots are tender but not at all mushy.

6   Uncover and stir in the herbs and spices. Cook gently, stirring, for a few moments. Stir in the tomato paste, the sultanas and their wine. Stir in the minced beef and the squeezed bulghur. Season to taste. Stir and cook for a minute or so.

7   Pile about 2 tablespoons of filling into each pepper half. Cover and refrigerate at this point if desired.

8   Preheat the oven to 350° F, 180° C, Gas Mark 4. Cover the baking dish with foil, shiny side in. Bake for 30 minutes. Serve hot. Pass a jug of Yoghurt-Herb Sauce.

Yoghurt Herb Sauce

Stir a generous handful of chopped fresh coriander, mint and parsley into non-fat yoghurt.

VEAL-POTATO BALLS

Makes approximately 50 meatballs

Serve veal-potato balls in Red Pepper and Tomato Borscht (page 48), or serve on toothpicks on a buffet with New York Deli Mustard (page 138) for dipping.

2 egg whites	1 lb/480 g minced veal
Grated zest of ½ small lemon	4 fl oz/120 ml mashed potatoes (see page 108)
1 teaspoon chopped fresh dill	2 tablespoons chopped fresh parsley
½ teaspoon ground allspice	1 tablespoon drained capers in
Salt and a generous amount of	vinegar, chopped
freshly ground pepper to taste	4 cloves garlic, minced

1   Lightly beat the egg whites with the lemon zest, dill, allspice, salt and pepper. Add to the veal with the remaining ingredients. Combine well with your hands. Fry a tiny piece in a small non-stick frying pan and taste, then adjust seasonings to your liking.
2   Preheat the grill. Line the grill tray with foil, shiny side out.
3   Form the mixture into small balls, smaller than walnuts but a little larger than marbles.
4   Place the meatballs 1–2 inches/2.5–5 cm from the heat and grill for 2 minutes on one side and 3 minutes on the second side. Blot on paper towels.

❄ LAMB MEATBALLS FOR COUSCOUS

Makes approximately 35 meatballs

These spicy little morsels are perfect with Couscous with Vegetables (page 101) or on their own.

1 lb/480 g lean minced lamb	1 rounded tablespoon tomato paste
1 small aubergine, baked, peeled and chopped fine (see page 21)	2 teaspoons ground cumin
	1 teaspoon ground coriander
3 cloves garlic, crushed	½ teaspoon ground cayenne
4 tablespoons chopped mint or parsley or a mixture	4 fl oz/120 ml wholemeal breadcrumbs
	Salt and freshly ground pepper to taste

1   Place minced lamb in a bowl. Add remaining ingredients. Mix with your hands until thoroughly amalgamated. Fry a tiny test piece (use no fat!) in a small, non-stick frying pan. Taste, then adjust seasonings in the meat to your liking.
2   Preheat the grill to its highest setting.
3   With your hands roll small balls, each a little smaller than a walnut. You will have approximately 35 in all. Line the grill pan with foil, shiny side up. Put a rack on the grill pan. Place the meatballs on the rack.
4   When the grill is very hot, grill the meatballs, 1 inch/2.5 cm from the heat, for 5–7 minutes, until browned on top and just cooked through (no need to turn them). Remove very gently, using tongs and a spatula. Blot on paper towels to eliminate any traces of fat, and serve. The meatballs may be made in advance and refrigerated. To reheat, place them in a shallow frying pan with some warm stock. Simmer gently, covered, for 5–7 minutes. (Don't boil. The surface of the stock should barely move.) Fish out very gently with a slotted spoon.

🕐 ✳ Bake the aubergine in the microwave.

CHEESE STUFFED
MEATBALLS

Makes 30 meatballs

Each meatball has a tender, gooey heart of melted Mozzarella cheese. These are excellent simmered in Tomato Sauce (page 16) for 30 minutes and served with pasta, Mashed Potatoes (page 108), or Polenta (page 114).

---

10 oz/300 g minced beef (very lean)	*3 tablespoons grated Parmesan*
2 medium aubergines, baked,	*cheese*
peeled and finely chopped (see	*½ teaspoon herbes de Provence*
page 21)	*Salt and pepper to taste*
2½ tablespoons brown breadcrumbs	*2½ oz/75 g Italian Mozzarella cheese*

---

1   Line a grill pan with foil, shiny side up. Put a rack on the grill pan. Preheat the grill to its highest setting.
2   Put the minced beef in a bowl. Add the aubergine, breadcrumbs, Parmesan cheese, herbs, salt and pepper. Mix very well with a fork or your hands. In a tiny frying pan, fry a tiny test piece, without using any fat. Taste and then adjust seasonings in the mixture to your liking.
3   Cut the Mozzarella cheese into 30 small pieces. Make the meatballs, enclosing a small piece of Mozzarella cheese in the centre of each. Roll each meatball thoroughly between the palms to enclose the Mozzarella cheese.
4   Arrange the meatballs on the grill rack. Grill for 3–5 minutes on one side, and 2–3 minutes on the second. Blot very well on paper towels.

Bake the aubergine in the microwave.

MARJORIE HOEK'S
'TAMALE PIE' MEATBALLS

Makes approximately 24 meatballs

This recipe won first prize in a Slim Cuisine recipe contest. I loved it and so did all my helpers and testers. I was impressed with the spicing, which is *very* Mexican. Unsweetened chocolate is used as a seasoning in many Mexican savoury dishes; cocoa powder, of course, is a lower-fat form of chocolate. Cornmeal (maize meal) is available in many wholefood and speciality food stores. If you can't find fine cornmeal, polenta will do. Meatballs may not be elegant, but they can be quite marvellous. Serve it for a family dinner or as the centrepiece for a Mexican party buffet.

Meatball ingredients
1 lb/480 g very lean minced beef
2 oz/60 g fine cornmeal
1 egg
1 onion, finely chopped or well
  minced
1 teaspoon cumin
1 teaspoon paprika
1 teaspoon fat-reduced cocoa powder
  (see page 155)
1 teaspoon thyme, fresh if possible

½ teaspoon cayenne or 1 mild fresh
  chilli, finely chopped

Sauce ingredients
1 (14 oz/420 g) tin chopped
  tomatoes
8 fl oz/240 ml fresh, strained orange
  juice
Freshly ground black pepper to taste
Handful of chopped parsley

1   Preheat oven to 180° F, 350° C, Gas Mark 4.
2   Mix all ingredients with your hands. They should be tho-
    roughly combined. Form into meatballs 1–1½ inches/2.5–4 cm
    in diameter. Place in one layer on a non-stick baking dish. Bake
    in the preheated oven until browned, 1½ hours or so.
3   Remove meatballs and blot on paper towels to eliminate
    rendered fat. Put the meatballs in a baking dish in one layer.
4   Combine sauce ingredients and pour over the meatballs.
    Return to the oven and bake uncovered until sauce is bubbly
    and tops of meatballs are well browned – about another
    30 minutes. Sprinkle with parsley and serve.

❄   # SAUSAGE PATTIES

Makes 30–35 sausage patties

Sausage meat keeps for a day or two in the fridge, or you may want
to form it into patties and freeze, to be used as needed. They make
lovely breakfast sausages. (Please don't say that aubergine sounds
peculiar as a breakfast ingredient. By now you know that baked
aubergine is the secret ingredient in Slim Cuisine sausages and
meatballs. It lessens the amount of meat in each sausage, provides
juiciness and leaves *no* aubergine taste.) Or they are excellent
surrounding that annual Christmas turkey.

1 lb/480 g lean minced pork
Chopped pulp of 1 Baked Aubergine
  (page 21)
Salt and freshly ground pepper to taste

1 teaspoon rubbed sage
¼ teaspoon allspice
Pinch of nutmeg

1   Combine all ingredients in a bowl. Use your hands to amalga-
    mate it thoroughly. Fry a tiny test piece in a little frying pan
    (use no fat!) and taste. Adjust seasoning.

2   Line the grill tray with foil, shiny side up. Place a rack on the grill tray. Preheat the grill.
3   Form the sausage mixture into balls, a little smaller than walnuts. Flatten into plump patties. Place on grill rack.
4   Grill, close to the heat, for 2 minutes. Turn each one carefully, and grill for an additional 2–3 minutes. Blot on a layer of paper towels and serve.

🕕 ⊠ Bake the aubergine in the microwave.

❄️
AUBERGINE-SAUSAGE SAUCE FOR PASTA

Makes 3 pts/1800 ml

This is an interesting and delicious variant of Bolognese sauce. I learned it years ago from the proprietor of a New York Italian restaurant. The original version was very high in fat; this one is not, but it manages to surpass the original in taste.

Sausage ingredients	Sauce ingredients
1 lb/480 g very lean minced pork	1 large Spanish onion, coarsely diced
Finely chopped flesh of 3 Baked Aubergines (see page 21)	1 red, 1 yellow pepper, cut into ½ inch/1.25 cm lengthwise strips, peeled
1 teaspoon fennel or anise seeds	16 fl oz/480 ml tinned sieved tomatoes
¼ teaspoon crushed dried chillies	4 large ripe summer tomatoes,
3 garlic cloves, crushed to a paste with a mallet	peeled, seeded, juiced and chopped or 14 oz/420 g tinned
4 tablespoons finely chopped fresh parsley	chopped tomatoes
3 tablespoons dry red wine	Chopped flesh of 2 additional Baked Aubergines (see page 21)
Salt and freshly ground pepper to taste	1 piece Parmesan rind

1   Combine the sausage ingredients in a large bowl and mix very well. Refrigerate, well covered, for a few hours. It can be kept, if necessary, for up to two days.
2   Combine sausage mix and chopped onion in a large, heavy frying pan. Cook, stirring, over moderate heat until the meat is thoroughly cooked and the onion is tender. Drain in a colander over a bowl. Blot the pan with paper towels.
3   When well drained, return to the pan. Stir in pepper strips. Stir and cook for about 3 minutes. Stir in remaining ingredients. Simmer, stirring occasionally, for 15 minutes or so, until the sauce is very thick and the peppers are tender. Serve tossed into freshly cooked pasta shells or rotini, or serve with Polenta (page 114).

Poultry

♡ ⊕ CHICKEN LIVER KEBABS

Makes 10 small skewers

Chinese five-spice powder and chilli and garlic sauce are available in most supermarkets and delicatessens. This is a very delicate and attractive way to serve chicken livers. Remember, liver, although low in fat and high in vitamins and minerals, is also high in cholesterol. Don't eat liver if your blood cholesterol level is high.

Marinade ingredients	Skewer ingredients
1 tablespoon teriyaki sauce	1 lb/480 g chicken livers, trimmed
1/4 teaspoon five-spice powder	and cut in halves
Zest of 1/2 orange	1 small red pepper, peeled and cut
Freshly ground pepper to taste	into 1 inch/2.5 cm squares
2 tablespoons sherry	1 small yellow pepper, peeled and
1 teaspoon chilli and garlic sauce	cut into 1 inch/2.5 cm squares
	1 box cherry tomatoes

1   In a bowl, stir together teriyaki sauce, five-spice powder, orange zest, freshly ground pepper, sherry, and chilli and garlic sauce. Add the livers and stir well. Cover and leave to marinate at room temperature for 1 hour.

2   Preheat the grill to its highest point. Line the grill tray with foil, shiny side up, and place the rack on the grill tray.

3   Drain the livers and reserve the marinade. Using ten 4 inch/10 cm metal skewers, thread the chicken livers as follows: a pepper square, a liver half, a cherry tomato, a liver half, a

pepper square, a liver half, a pepper square, a cherry tomato. Repeat until all the skewers are filled.

4   Grill, about 3 inches/8 cm from the heat, for 4–6 minutes altogether. Turn the skewers and baste with the marinade, using a pastry brush, about every 2 minutes. Do not overcook. The livers should be *just* cooked through and not dried out. Serve at once with rice, Kasha (see page 132), or Wheat Pilaf (see page 134).

♡   # ROAST TURKEY

I turkeyed out years ago. It was Thanksgiving that did it. Year after year, late November arrived yet again, and with it the obligatory meal of the mythic big brown bird and its accompanying sub-mythic vegetables. Ben Franklin campaigned for the turkey to be America's national bird. Had he succeeded, Americans would probably have spent the last 213 Novembers devouring roast eagle with all the trimmings, and I would have experienced an eagle crisis instead. Anyway, I serve shepherd's pie on Thanksgiving now. (Don't laugh. You haven't lived until you've tried my shepherd's pie – see page 75.) I found out that even though I opted out of the November turkey game, I was allowed to keep my citizenship. Indeed, except for this aberration I consider myself a good (though expatriate) American. But I digress. The point is that the British are caught in the turkey trap too, but it happens here in December. Turkeys are lean, but the fatty excesses that are committed upon them in the name of Christmas are appalling. Here is a delicious low-fat method of serving up the festive bird.

15–18 lb/7.2–8.64 kg free-range turkey	3 tablespoons Dijon mustard
1 lemon	1 tablespoon grated Parmesan cheese
8 fl oz/240 ml chopped fresh parsley	6 Spanish onions
4 cloves minced garlic	Stock
3 small onions, minced	Cognac
2 tablespoons chopped fresh rosemary	

---

1   Have the fresh turkey at room temperature. Remove giblets and use to make turkey stock. Save the liver for another use. Wash turkey inside and out and rub it inside with a cut lemon. Preheat oven to 325° F, 170° C, Gas Mark 3.

2   Loosen the skin on the turkey's breast. Combine parsley, garlic, minced onion, rosemary, Dijon mustard and Parmesan cheese. Spread the mixture over the breast, under the skin.

87

3   Stuff the large cavity of the bird with 3 large Spanish onions, quartered. Plug up opening with a ball of foil. Secure the neck flap of skin with a skewer. Secure the wings to the body with skewers. Do not truss legs. (The heat will penetrate to the thighs more efficiently if the legs are left free.)

4   Place turkey, breast down, on a rack in a roasting pan in the preheated oven. Put some stock and a small amount of cognac in the pan. Slice 3 onions into the pan. Roast, breast down, for a little more than half the cooking time. Then turn the breast up for remainder of time. Baste the bird with stock and a bit of cognac every 20 minutes or so. Replenish stock as it evaporates. If the turkey browns too fast, drape it with clean cheesecloth and baste through the cloth.

5   When a thermometer inserted into the thickest part of the breast registers 170 to 175 degrees, the turkey is done. (Use an instant-read thermometer, if possible.) An overcooked bird is dry and tasteless, so check the temperature carefully. An 18 lb/8 kg bird will be done in about 4½ hours, but turkeys are unpredictable. Depend on your thermometer; use the clock only as a guide. When finished, let the turkey rest for 30 minutes.

6   While the bird is resting, pour the pan juices into a jug and place in the freezer so the fat rises to the top. Skim off *all* fat and pour the juices back into the roasting pan. Place the pan on the stove. Add a bit more stock if necessary and 4 fl oz/120 ml cognac. Boil down rapidly, stirring, and scraping up the browned bits. Strain the gravy or not, as you wish.

7   Discard the turkey skin (too much fat) and the stuffing under the skin (its purpose was to keep the breast meat moist and flavourful). Serve with the gravy and Chestnut Stuffing (see following recipe).

'The fact was, none of them cared for turkey. Still . . . it didn't seem right to serve anything else. It would just feel wrong.'

Anne Tyler, *The Accidental Tourist*

CHESTNUT STUFFING

To accompany a large roast turkey

It's best to bake this in a separate casserole, rather than in the cavity of the bird, so that it does not absorb an inordinate amount of fat. And the turkey will be juicier if roasted without stuffing.

Sausage Mix (see recipe below)
2 large onions, chopped
1 large tin (2 lb/960 g cooked, shelled chestnuts, drained and rinsed
8 fl oz/240 ml chopped fresh parsley
1 teaspoon fresh thyme or ¼–½ teaspoon dried thyme
1 small Baked Aubergine, chopped fine (see page 21)
1 rounded tablespoon tomato paste

5 oz/150 g French bread, torn into pieces and toasted lightly in the oven
Approximately 4 fl oz/120 ml skimmed milk
Salt and pepper to taste
Pinch or two of cayenne pepper to taste
4 fl oz/120 ml cognac
8 fl oz/240 ml de-fatted turkey or chicken stock

1   Brown fresh Sausage Mix and onions in a heavy non-stick frying pan. Break up meat as it cooks. Drain off all fat.
2   Mash chestnuts and add to meat and onions. Add parsley, thyme, Baked Aubergine and tomato paste.
3   Moisten toasted bread with milk. Squeeze out excess. Place in a large bowl with chestnut mixture. Add salt, peppers and cognac and toss it all together. Taste and adjust seasonings. It should have a lively, peppery taste.
4   Put into a large gratin dish, pour in the stock, cover and bake at 325° F, 170° C, Gas Mark 3, for 1 hour. Uncover and bake for 1 additional hour.

Sausage Mix

1 lb/480 g lean minced veal
1 small Baked Aubergine, chopped fine (see page 21)
4 fl oz/120 ml dry breadcrumbs

Juice and grated zest of ½ small lemon
6 tablespoons freshly grated Parmesan cheese
Salt and pepper to taste

Combine thoroughly.

ROAST CHICKEN

Serves 3–4

Use a free-range chicken, a corn-fed one, or a Poulet Noir. The method of stuffing a savoury mixture under the breast skin produces a remarkably succulent and savoury bird. Discard the stuffing and the skin (too much fat) before serving.

1 3–3½ lb/1.44–1.68 kg chicken	*1 tablespoon Dijon mustard*
8 fl oz/240 ml chopped parsley	*1 tablespoon grated Parmesan*
4 cloves garlic, minced	*1 Spanish onion, cut in half and*
1 small onion, minced	*sliced into thick half-moons*
2 tablespoons chopped fresh	*Chicken stock*
rosemary	*4 fl oz/120 ml white wine*

1   Preheat oven to 375° F, 190° C, Gas Mark 5.
2   Loosen the skin on the chicken's breast. Combine remaining ingredients except Spanish onion, stock and wine. Spread this mixture over the breast, under the skin.
3   Spread out the Spanish onion slices in a roasting pan. Place a rack across the pan. Place the chicken, breast up, on the rack. Pour in 4 fl oz/120 ml stock and the wine.
4   Roast for 1¼–1½ hours, basting with the pan juices and additional stock, if necessary, every 15 minutes. Turn the chicken occasionally, so that it cooks evenly.
5   Remove the chicken from the roasting pan and allow to rest on a plate, loosely covered with foil. Thoroughly de-grease the pan juices.
6   Return the pan juices to the roasting pan and put the pan right on to the hob. Bring to the boil, scraping up the browned bits with a wooden spoon.
7   Discard the skin and the stuffing from the chicken. Serve the chicken with the pan juices.

PIQUANT CHICKEN

Makes 8 pieces

I love this way of cooking chicken; it tastes so *fattening*! The mixture of yoghurt and mustard keeps the chicken meltingly tender and moist, but the taste is not at all yoghurty.

8 fl oz/240 ml yoghurt	*8 chicken thighs, skinned*
4 tablespoons Dijon mustard	*8 tablespoons wholemeal*
Salt and freshly ground pepper to	*breadcrumbs*
taste	

1   Preheat oven to 375° F, 190° C, Gas Mark 5.
2   Mix together the yoghurt, mustard, salt and pepper.
3   Combine yoghurt mixture and chicken in a non-reactive dish that will hold them in one layer. Refrigerate for 12–24 hours.
4   Line two baking trays with foil, shiny side up. Put a rack on each tray.

5   Put each piece of chicken, skinned side up, on the rack. They should be thoroughly coated with the yoghurt mixture. Sprinkle each piece with a tablespoon of crumbs.

6   Bake for 40–50 minutes, or until just done.

TANDOORI CHICKEN

Makes 8 pieces

This, as does the previous Piquant Chicken, seems to please everyone. It can be served hot or cold, and makes a wonderful addition to a party buffet.

8 chicken drumsticks, skinned	*Pinch of ground cloves*
Salt and freshly ground pepper to	*¼ teaspoon ground cinnamon*
taste	*¼–½ teaspoon cayenne pepper*
1 tablespoon ground coriander	*12 fl oz/360 ml yoghurt*
1 teaspoon ground cumin	*6 cloves garlic, peeled and crushed*
1 teaspoon ground turmeric	*1 onion, chopped*
1 teaspoon garam masala	*1 piece ginger (1 inch/2.5 cm),*
¼ teaspoon nutmeg	*peeled and minced*

1   Slash each chicken drumstick in two places. Toss with salt and pepper. Set aside.

2   Combine remaining ingredients. Mix chicken with this mixture in a large bowl, cover, and allow to marinate in the refrigerator overnight.

3   Preheat oven to 350° F, 180° C, Gas Mark 4. Spread chicken pieces out in one layer in a shallow baking dish. Brush with some of the marinade. Cover tightly with foil. Bake for 30 minutes.

4   Uncover. Bake for 20–30 minutes more or until just done, but very moist. Remove from pan. Pour juices into a jug. Refrigerate the juices. Wipe out the baking dish.

5   Arrange the chicken pieces in the dish in one layer. Grill 2½–3 inches/6.5–8 cm from the grilling element for approximately 2 minutes on each side, until nicely browned. Serve at once.

6   When the juices are cold, scrape out and discard hardened fat. Use the flavourful stock for sautéeing or soups.

CHICKEN WITH MANGO SAUCE

Serves 4

The ultimate dinner party dish, when you want to impress your guests. In fact you'll knock their socks off.

4 chicken breasts of equal size, skinned but not boned	4 tablespoon mango chutney
2 large onions, cut in half and sliced into thin half-moons	Salt and freshly ground pepper to taste
8 fl oz/240 ml chicken stock	Pinch nutmeg
2 mangoes, peeled and chopped	Zest and juice of 1 lime

1   Preheat oven to 350° F, 180° C, Gas Mark 4.
2   Sauté chicken breasts skinned side down, in a non-stick pan, until lightly browned. Set aside on a plate lined with paper towels. Blot well. Blot out any fat from the frying pan, but do not rub off any browned bits.
3   Put the onion and 3 fl oz/90 ml of stock in the pan. Cover and boil for 3–5 minutes. Uncover and stir, scraping up any browned bits in the pan. Stir in the mangoes, the chutney, and seasoning except the lime juice and zest. Simmer for 5 minutes.
4   Put the chicken, skinned side up, in a baking dish. Pour the mango mixture over the pieces. Cover and bake for 45 minutes or until the chicken is tender. Remove the chicken to a plate, cover loosely with foil and keep warm.
5   De-grease the pan juices. Purée them in the liquidizer. Correct seasonings. Pour over and around the chicken and serve at once.

LEMON ROASTED CHICKEN

Serves 4

This was inspired by a winning recipe in the *Daily Mail*'s Slim Cuisine recipe contest. I don't know which is better, the moist chicken meat, or the incredible gravy. Leftovers make superb sandwiches.

Juice of 1½ lemons	1 medium (2½–3 lb/1.2–1.44 kg roasting chicken, trimmed of fat
1 teaspoon black pepper	
2 teaspoons cumin	4–6 fl oz/120–180 ml dry white wine
1 teaspoon paprika or paprika paste	

1   Mix the lemon juice with all the ingredients except chicken and wine. Make small incisions all over the chicken (except in the breast) and rub in the lemon mixture. Loosen the breast skin and rub the lemon mixture under the skin. Place the squeezed lemon halves in the chicken's cavity. Marinate overnight.
2   Next day, preheat the oven to 450° F, 230° C, Gas Mark 8. Place a rack across a flameproof shallow roasting pan. Place chicken on the rack and roast breast down for 15 minutes, breast up for approximately 45 minutes until just done.
3   Allow the chicken to rest on a plate, loosely covered with foil. Tilt the roasting pan, and prop it in the tilted position. With a large spoon, spoon out all fat (there will be plenty) and discard. Put the roasting pan right on the hob, and turn the heat on full. Stir and scrape up the drippings and browned bits. Pour in 4–6 fl oz/120–180 ml dry white wine. Boil, stirring and scraping, until you have a dark, thick, rich sauce, and the alcohol has cooked away. Serve this powerful juice with the carved chicken.

CHICKEN PESTO POTATO SALAD

Makes 2¾ pts/1680 ml

Make this main dish potato salad the star of an elegant summer buffet. Begin with Gazpacho (page 55) and conclude with Strawberries in Raspberry Sauce (page 141) and a cloud of fromage frais.

1 lb/480 g small new potatoes	4 fl oz/120 ml Slim Cuisine Pesto
1 lb/480 g boned and cubed smoked chicken	(see page 17)
	2 fl oz/60 ml buttermilk
1 red pepper, peeled and coarsely chopped	Whole basil leaves

1   Cut the potatoes into halves or quarters, depending on size. Do not peel. Steam over boiling water until cooked through but not mushy. Cool. When cool, cut into 1 inch/2.5 cm chunks.
2   Combine potatoes, chicken and peppers. Thin Pesto to dressing consistency with a bit of buttermilk. Toss the potato-chicken mixture with the Pesto. Serve on a plate, garnished with whole basil leaves.

ORIENTAL CHICKEN SALAD

Makes 2 pts/1200 ml

One of my best cold party buffet dishes. Don't add the mango until the last minute, or it will cause the chicken to develop a rubbery texture.

6 boned, skinned chicken breast
  halves
1 large onion, chopped
2 cloves garlic, minced
A 1 inch/2.5 cm piece fresh ginger,
  peeled and minced
Seeds of 5 cardamom pods
2 tablespoons soy sauce
2½ tablespoons dry sherry
2 tablespoons honey
3–4 fl oz/90–120 ml sherry, wine
  vinegar, or rice wine vinegar

Salt and freshly ground pepper to
  taste
1 small red pepper, peeled and
  chopped
1 stalk celery, cut in half lengthwise
  and thinly sliced
1 mango, peeled and cubed

Garnish
1 sliced Granny Smith apple,
  rubbed with lemon juice
Fresh coriander or parsley

1 Preheat oven to 350° F, 180° C, Gas Mark 4.
2 Trim the chicken breasts of any bits of gristle and fat. Spread in one layer in a heavy, very shallow baking dish, skinned side up.
3 Combine onion, garlic, ginger, cardamom seeds, soy sauce, sherry and honey. Bring to the boil.
4 Pour this mixture evenly over the chicken. Cover tightly with foil. Bake for 30 minutes or until the chicken is *just* done.
5 Put the chicken in one layer on a plate. Cover loosely with cling film or foil. Pour and scrape the onions and juices into a saucepan.
6 Boil the juices until they are syrupy and the onions are amber and tender.
7 Cut the chicken into ½ inch/1.25 cm cubes. Sprinkle with the vinegar and toss together. Gently stir in the onion mixture. Season to taste with salt and pepper. Spread out in a shallow dish, cover and set aside.
8 Just before serving, stir in the pepper, celery and mango. Arrange attractively in a bowl or on a serving plate. Garnish with the apple slices and coriander or parsley. Serve at room temperature.

Vegetarian

'Since he was not a man who easily showed his liking for people, he chose to cook them their favourite foods instead – the comfort foods that everyone turns to when he is feeling low.'

Anne Tyler, *Searching for Caleb*

GRATIN OF RED BEANS, NEW ORLEANS STYLE

Serves 6

A colourful and spicy bean feast, to serve as a main dish or a vegetable accompaniment.

---

3 large onions, coarsely chopped	1 tin (14 oz/420 g) chopped tomatoes
8 fl oz/240 ml stock	
4 red peppers, peeled and coarsely chopped	1 bay leaf
	Salt and freshly ground pepper to taste
4 stalks celery, chopped	
½ teaspoon cumin	4 fl oz/120 ml red wine
½ teaspoon coriander	2 tins (15 oz/450 g each) red kidney beans, drained and rinsed
Pinch of cayenne pepper	
½ teaspoon dried thyme	2 tablespoons dry wholemeal breadcrumbs
¼ teaspoon dried oregano, crumbled	2 tablespoons grated Parmesan cheese

---

1   Preheat oven to 400° F, 200° C, Gas Mark 6.
2   Put the onions in a frying pan with 6 fl oz/180 ml of stock.

Cover. Boil for 5 minutes. Uncover, reduce heat somewhat, and simmer until amber brown and beginning to stick to the pan.

3 Stir in the peppers, celery and a splash of stock. Stir and cook until the added vegetables are softened.
4 Stir in the cumin, coriander, cayenne pepper, thyme, oregano, tomatoes, bayleaf, salt and pepper and wine. Simmer, stirring occasionally, for 20–30 minutes, until thick and savoury.
5 Stir in the beans. Spread in a baking dish. Sprinkle with a mixture of the breadcrumbs and the grated cheese. (The recipe can be prepared to this point and refrigerated until needed.)
6 Bake the beans, uncovered, for 30 minutes, until bubbling and browned on top.

♡ Omit cheese.

 # BLACK BEANS

Makes 2½ pts/1500 ml

1 lb/480 g dried black beans, washed and picked over 6½ pts/3900 ml water (see note)	Pinch of ground cloves
	¼ teaspoon ground allspice
	½ teaspoon ground coriander
1 large Spanish onion, chopped	Pinch or two of cayenne pepper
10 fl oz/300 ml stock	3¼ pts/1950 ml stock
4 cloves garlic, peeled	Freshly ground pepper to taste
½ teaspoon ground cumin	

1 In a cool part of the kitchen soak the beans overnight in 3¼ pts/1950 ml of water. On the next day, drain them.
2 Spread onion pieces on the bottom of a heavy saucepan. Heat until they sizzle and begin to stick to the pan. Pour in stock and stir in garlic and all seasonings. Simmer, stirring occasionally, until the mixture is thick and the onions and spices are 'frying' in their own juices. When the onions are tender, dump in the drained beans.
3 Stir in 3¼ pts/1950 ml stock. Cover and simmer for 1 hour.
4 Season to taste with salt and pepper. Simmer for an additional hour or more, until very tender. Taste and adjust seasonings.

BLACK BEAN CHILAQUILES

Serves 8

Chilaquiles are a sort of Mexican lasagne: tortilla pieces layered with sauce and cheese, and sometimes bits of poultry as well. There are many versions. If you don't want to bother soaking and cooking the dried beans, substitute 3 tins of red kidney beans. Traditionally, chilaquiles are made with tortilla pieces that have been deep fried. In my version, the tortillas are baked. Since baked tortillas are a compelling and healthy snack, as well as a component of chilaquiles, it pays to bake up a huge batch every once in a while, and store them in a biscuit tin until needed.

12 corn tortillas (see page 98)
1 onion, chopped
10 fl oz/300 ml stock
3 cloves garlic, crushed
½ teaspoon cayenne pepper
½ teaspoon ground cumin seed
½ teaspoon chilli powder
Black Beans (see page 96)

16 fl oz/480 ml Tomato Sauce (see page 16), flavoured with a pinch each of cayenne and cumin
8 oz/240 g Mozzarella cheese, finely shredded
6 tablespoons Parmesan cheese
Chopped fresh coriander
Lime wedges

1 Preheat oven to 300° F, 150° C, Gas Mark 2.
2 Bake the tortillas directly on the oven shelf, for 15–20 minutes, turning once until crisp right through (they will break with a clean 'snap'). Break into coarse pieces and set aside.
3 Spread onion pieces out in a heavy frying pan. Cook over moderate heat, without stirring, until the onions are sizzling and beginning to stick to the pan. Stir in the stock and let it bubble up, stirring up the browned deposits in the pan with the wooden spoon as it bubbles. Stir in the garlic and spices. Turn the heat down and simmer, stirring frequently, until the mixture is thick (not at all soupy) and the onions and spices are 'frying' in their own juices. Don't rush this step, it is essential that the spices should not have a harsh raw taste.
4 Stir in the Black Beans and heat gently. Mash roughly, while still in the pan, with a potato masher. You want a rough lumpy mixture, not a smooth purée. Set aside.
5 In a gratin dish spread a layer of ⅓ of the tortilla pieces. Spread ⅓ of the Black Beans over the tortillas, and spread ⅓ of the Tomato Sauce over the Black Beans. Sprinkle with ⅓ of the cheeses. Repeat order. End with the remaining Tomato Sauce, Black Beans, tortillas, and cheeses.
6 Bake for 30 minutes, covered. Uncover and bake for 5–10 minutes more. Serve garnished with lime wedges.

Tortillas

Tortillas are thin maize pancakes made from *masa* (lime-treated maize meal). I learned to make tortillas according to ancient tradition at the hacienda of an Aztec farming family in a remote Mexican town. Guadalupe, my hostess, lived in the hacienda that had been in her family for generations. She taught me to make tortillas as she makes them every day of her life; indeed, as all her female ancestors have done since before the conquest. For my tortilla lesson I knelt on the cold, hard floor of a stone-walled, high-ceilinged room next to the cow enclosure and pig pens. In front of me, a brisk fire of corn cobs and twigs blazed under a large clay griddle; to the side, a wet pile of *masa* waited on a tilted three-legged slab of volcanic rock. I was directed to pull off a lump of *masa*, flatten it into shape in a wooden tortilla press, pat it a few times, ease it on to the red-hot griddle, flip it over to bake the other side, then toss it into a napkin-lined basket. When Guadalupe did it, it seemed so simple: her movements were graceful and the whole process looked easy and languorous. But when I tried, it was not easy it all; the floor was punishingly hard, the griddle blister-ingly hot and the tortilla press supremely uninterested in pressing the dough evenly for me. Guadalupe stood on the sidelines utter-ing commands, her mouth twitching in amusement at my awkwardness. Her tortillas were perfectly round, smooth, even discs. Mine were lopsided, uneven in thickness and uneven at the edges. How happy I am to tell you that these ornery but delicious things are available in tins. Just wield the tin opener, shake them out and toast in the oven. They do not, I hasten to add, begin to match the thinness, elegance and all-round excellence of Guada-lupe's tortillas, but they sure are a convenience. And if you have a good Mexican or Latin American restaurant near your town, you may be able to buy fresh or frozen corn tortillas at a minimal price. I have done this successfully at Los Andes in Birmingham, Los Bandidos in Cambridge and Café Pacifico in London. It's certainly worth a try.

♡ ⏱ ❄ **SPICY BEAN SAUCE FOR PASTA**

Makes 2½ pts/1500 ml

Pasta is the ultimate fast food. With a good supply on hand, and a lavish choice of ingredients in the larder and freezer, lovely simple meals are always possible.

---

1 large Spanish onion, coarsely chopped	½ teaspoon ground allspice
4 fl oz/120 ml stock	Garlic purée from Baked Garlic (see page 17), to taste (optional)
2 red peppers, peeled and coarsely chopped	2 tins (14 oz/420 g each) chopped tomatoes
2 stalks celery, sliced into ½ inch/1.25 cm pieces	1 piece Parmesan rind
2 fl oz/60 ml red wine	1 tin (15 oz/450 g) red kidney beans, drained and rinsed
1 teaspoon ground cumin	1 tablespoon drained capers
1 teaspoon dried thyme	Salt and freshly ground pepper to taste
1 teaspoon dried tarragon	
Pinch of cayenne pepper	

---

1   Put the onion in a frying pan with 4 fl oz/120 ml of stock. Cover. Boil for 5 minutes. Uncover, reduce heat somewhat and simmer until amber brown and beginning to stick to the pan.
2   Stir in the peppers, celery and the red wine. Stir and cook until the added vegetables are softened. With your wooden spoon, scrape up the browned bits on the bottom of the pan as you stir.
3   Stir in herbs, spices, optional garlic, tomatoes and Parmesan rind. Simmer, uncovered, for 30 minutes or so, stirring occasionally, until thickened and savoury. Stir in the beans and the capers. Season to taste. Simmer for 5–10 minutes more. Serve over corkscrew pasta.

Note: To make a pasta-bean casserole, mix this sauce with cooked (al dente) pasta, either rotini or penne. Sprinkle the top with shredded Italian Mozzarella cheese and freshly grated Parmesan cheese. Bake until the cheese is melted and bubbly.

❄ VEGETARIAN CHILAQUILES

Serves 6

Another variation on the 'Mexican lasagne' theme, this time with red and green peppers and plenty of sweet corn.

6 corn tortillas
1 large onion, chopped
1 red, 1 green pepper, peeled and
  chopped
1 chilli pepper, minced (a jalapeño
  chilli if possible)
6 fl oz/180 ml stock
1 teaspoon ground cumin
1 teaspoon ground coriander
Cayenne pepper to taste
½ teaspoon mild chilli powder
2 cloves garlic, crushed

3 tins (14 oz/420 g each) chopped
  tomatoes
Parmesan cheese rind
2 tablespoons tomato paste
Salt to taste
Pinch of sugar (optional)
12 oz/360 g frozen sweet corn (no
  need to thaw completely)
7 tablespoons grated Parmesan
  cheese
4 oz/120 g Mozzarella cheese,
  shredded

1 Preheat oven to 300° F, 100° C, Gas Mark 2.
2 Bake the tortillas directly on the oven shelf for 15–20 minutes, turning once, until crisp right through. Break into coarse pieces and set aside.
3 Put the onion, peppers, chilli, stock, spices, and garlic in a heavy, non-reactive frying pan. Cover and bring to the boil. Boil for 5 minutes. Uncover, reduce heat and simmer for a few minutes more until the onion is tender and browned.
4 Stir in tomatoes and add cheese rind. Simmer, uncovered, for 20 minutes. Add tomato paste and simmer for 5 minutes. Add salt to taste, and a pinch of sugar if it is too acidic. Discard cheese rind.
5 In a shallow, non-reactive gratin dish or baking dish, layer ⅓ of the tortilla pieces, ⅓ of the sauce, ⅓ of the corn, ⅓ of the cheeses. Repeat twice.
6 Bake uncovered for 35 minutes, until bubbly. Serve at once.

Ⓢ PASTA WITH CREAMY FENNEL SAUCE

Serves 8

You will want to dive headfirst into this glorious bowl of pasta, and wallow. Why would anyone want to eat high-butterfat pasta dishes, when low-fat food can taste so outrageously good?

½ lb/240 g quark, at room
  temperature
1 oz/30 g pine nuts
5 tablespoons grated Parmesan
  cheese
Purée from 1–2 heads Baked Garlic
  (see page 17)

3 peppers (1 each red, green,
  yellow), peeled and coarsely
  chopped
2 large cloves garlic, coarsely
  chopped
1 teaspoon dried tarragon,
  crumbled

3 medium onions, coarsely chopped
8 oz/240 g white mushrooms,
  quartered
8 oz/240 g chestnut (brown)
  mushrooms, quartered
1 head fennel, trimmed and sliced
  (cut each slice in half)

½ teaspoon dried thyme, crumbled
Salt and freshly ground pepper to
  taste
8 fl oz/240 ml stock
4 fl oz/120 ml red wine
2 dashes soy sauce
1 lb/480 g pasta quills
4 fl oz/120 ml Tomato Sauce,
  unpuréed (see page 16)

1   Place quark, pine nuts, Parmesan cheese and Baked Garlic in
    the container of the food processor. Process until smooth and
    well blended. Set aside.
2   In a heavy, deep, non-reactive frying pan, combine the
    onions, mushrooms, fennel, peppers, chopped garlic, season-
    ings, stock, wine and soy sauce. Stir to combine very well.
    Bring to the boil. Simmer briskly, uncovered, stirring oc-
    casionally, until the vegetables are tender, and the liquid is
    greatly reduced and syrupy. Lower the heat a bit and cook
    gently, stirring occasionally, as the vegetables 'fry' in their
    own juices. When the liquid is almost gone, set aside.
3   Cook the quills in plenty of salted boiling water. Have a warm
    bowl ready. Warm the Tomato Sauce.
4   When the pasta is done, drain it well and toss it in the warm
    bowl with the cheese mixture. When the pasta is thoroughly
    coated, toss in the vegetable mixture and the Tomato Sauce.
    Rush to the table and serve *at once*.

♡   COUSCOUS WITH
                VEGETABLES

Makes 2 pts/1200 ml couscous, 3 pts/1800 ml vegetables

A fragrant vegetable curry surrounding a fluffy mound of couscous
looks so pretty and tastes so good. To make this a gala party meal,
add Lamb Meatballs (page 82), Piquant Chicken (page 90) and
Stufatino (page 70), and arrange it all attractively on a huge plate.

♡ ❋ Vegetable curry ingredients
    1 large Spanish onion, coarsely
      chopped
    24 fl oz/720 ml chicken stock
    3 celery stalks, sliced into
      ½ inch/1.25 cm pieces
    3 carrots, peeled and coarsely
      chopped

¼ teaspoon allspice
½ teaspoon ground ginger
1 teaspoon ground turmeric
1½ teaspoons ground coriander
¼ teaspoon ground cayenne pepper
1 teaspoon paprika or paprika paste
1 lb/480 g courgettes, sliced into
  ½ inch/1.25 cm pieces

4 cloves garlic, minced
3 small turnips, peeled and coarsely
   chopped
1 red, 1 green, 1 yellow pepper,
   peeled and coarsely chopped
1 head fennel – trim off tough outer
   layers and slice into half-inch/
   1.25 cm pieces
1½ teaspoons ground cumin

1 tin (15 oz/450 g) chick peas,
   drained
6 tablespoons fresh lemon juice
4 fl oz/120 ml chopped fresh parsley
2 fl oz/60 ml chopped fresh
   coriander

♡ ⊕ Couscous ingredients
¾ lb/360 g couscous
16 fl oz/480 ml boiling stock

---

1   Spread onion pieces out in a frying pan. Cook over moderate
    heat until the onions are sizzling and sticking to the pan. Stir in
    10 fl oz/300 ml of stock and let it bubble up, stirring up the
    browned deposits in the pan as it bubbles. Stir in celery,
    carrots, garlic, turnips, peppers, fennel and all spices. Turn
    the heat down a bit and simmer, stirring frequently until the
    mixture is thick (not at all soupy) and the vegetables and spices
    are 'frying' in their own juices.
2   Stir in the remaining vegetable curry ingredients, including
    the remaining 14 fl oz/420 ml stock. Season to taste with salt
    and freshly ground pepper. Simmer gently, covered, for 15
    minutes.
3   Combine couscous with 16 fl oz/480 ml boiling stock in a large
    bowl. Let steep for 10–15 minutes, until the liquid is absorbed
    and the grains are tender. Fluff with a fork.
4   Serve the couscous in a mound on a large plate surrounded by
    the vegetables, or vice versa.

Omit chick peas. Substitute – if desired – drained, quartered
artichoke hearts, or fresh cauliflower florets. Eat the curry
without the couscous.

Couscous

Couscous, tiny grains of semolina, is available in cellophane pack-
ages in many supermarkets and wholefood shops. Most packaged
couscous is pre-cooked; it only needs a brief steeping in hot liquid.
The traditional method of cooking couscous involves at least two
steamings in a special couscousière, and can take up to an hour, so
the pre-cooked supermarket and wholefood store version is a great
boon to busy cooks. Couscous purists sneer at the pre-cooked
stuff, but I find it perfectly acceptable, and have used it as the focal
point of many happy dinner parties. It also can be used to make a
glorious pudding (see page 153).

'The Glaoui is one of the world's foremost manipulators of cous-cous balls. We watched him fascinated. He picks up a handful of the hot grain, tosses this in his palm without touching it with his fingers, and gently bounces it in the hollow of his hand until by some miracle it forms into a cohesive ball; this he then pops into his mouth, catching it on the fly. It was like watching a man with one hand make and eat golf balls.'

John Gunther, *Inside Africa*

⏲ ❄ VEGETARIAN CHILLI

Makes 3½ pts/2100 ml

Although I love good beef, I believe that my vegetarian chilli is better than any carnivore's chilli you might try. The faint-hearted may cut down on the amount of chilli powder, but if you use the full 5 tablespoons of *mild* I think you will find the dish not at all overpowering or incendiary.

---

6 fl oz/180 ml bulghur
18 fl oz/540 ml vegetable stock, brought to the boil
1 Spanish onion, coarsely chopped
3 celery stalks, sliced ½ inch/1.25 cm thick
3 carrots, peeled and coarsely chopped
4 cloves garlic, minced
5 tablespoons chilli powder (half hot, half mild, or to taste)
2 teaspoons ground cumin
1 red pepper, peeled and coarsely chopped
1 yellow pepper, peeled and coarsely chopped

1 green pepper, peeled and coarsely chopped
2 tins (14 oz/420 g each) chopped tomatoes
1 tin (15 oz/450 g) red kidney beans, drained
1 tin (15 oz/450 g) chick peas, drained
1 large cauliflower, trimmed and cut into florets
Salt and freshly ground pepper to taste

Garnishes
Fromage frais
Grated Parmesan cheese
Chopped fresh coriander

---

1 Combine the bulghur and 8 fl oz/240 ml hot stock in a bowl. Cover and set aside.
2 Spread the onions out in a heavy frying pan. Cook over moderate heat, without stirring, for 7–10 minutes, until the onions are sizzling and beginning to stick to the pan. Stir in 10 fl oz/300 ml of stock and let it bubble up, stirring up the browned deposits in the pan with a wooden spoon as it bubbles. Stir in the celery, carrot, garlic, chilli powder, cumin and peppers. Turn the heat down a bit and simmer, stirring

103

frequently, until the mixture is very thick (not at all soupy) and the vegetables and spices are 'frying' in their own juices. Don't rush this step, it is essential that the spices should not have a harsh, raw taste. Taste, and cook very gently for a few more minutes if necessary.

3   Stir in tomatoes, bulghur, kidney beans, chick peas, cauli-flower and salt and pepper. Simmer for 30 minutes, until the mixture is thick and the cauliflower is tender, but not mushy. This chilli may be made a day in advance and reheated gently at serving time. Serve with small bowls of the garnishes.

♡   Omit Parmesan cheese garnish.

❄ VEGETARIAN LASAGNE

Serves 6

Lasagne is no longer considered sophisticated, but watch the faces of your guests light up with joy when you ferry one – hot, steamy and odorous – to the table.

½ lb/240 g thinly julienned carrots	1½ lb/720 g spinach, washed,
½ lb/240 g thinly julienned red	stemmed and torn into strips, or
peppers	1½ lb/720 g frozen chopped
1 lb/480 g mushrooms, quartered	spinach
2 large onions, chopped	1 lb/480 g low-fat quark
8 fl oz/240 ml dry white wine	5–6 oz/150–180 g medium-fat
18 fl oz/540 ml vegetable stock	Mozzarella cheese, shredded
Several dashes soy sauce	6 tablespoons grated Parmesan
1½ teaspoons dried tarragon	cheese
½ teaspoon ground allspice	5 tablespoons skimmed milk
2 tablespoons tomato paste	5 oz/150 g lasagne noodles (the type
2 tablespoons chopped parsley	that need no pre-cooking)
Salt and freshly ground pepper to	
taste	

1   Combine the carrots, peppers, mushrooms, onions, wine, 8 fl oz/240 ml of stock, soy sauce, tarragon and ¼ teaspoon allspice in a heavy, deep, non-reactive frying pan. Simmer briskly, stirring occasionally, until the mixture is thick and the vegetables are tender. Stir in the tomato paste and parsley. Season with salt and pepper.

2   Cook the spinach in the water clinging to its leaves, until it is just limp. Drain and squeeze as dry as possible. If frozen spinach is being used, just drain it and squeeze as dry as possible. Season the spinach with a bit of salt and pepper and ¼ teaspoon allspice.

3   Mix together the quark, the Mozzarella cheese, 4 tablespoons of Parmesan cheese and the skimmed milk.
4   Pour 3–4 fl oz/90–120 ml of warm stock on to the surface of a non-reactive 8½ × 10 inch/21.5 × 25 cm baking dish. Pour 2–3 fl oz/90–120 ml of additional warm stock in a shallow dish and keep it at hand. Place a single layer of lasagne noodles in the 8½ × 10 inch/21.5 × 25 cm baking dish. Turn to thoroughly wet them with the stock. Spread the spinach over the noodle layer. Dip more lasagne noodles in the warm stock you have kept at hand and put on an even layer on the spinach.
5   Spread the cheese mixture on the noodles. Dip more noodles in the stock and put on an even layer over the cheese. Spread half the vegetable mixture on the layer, top with more wet noodles. Spread on the remaining vegetables. Spread the remaining cheese over the top, mixing it in with the vegetables as you spread. Sprinkle evenly with 2 tablespoons of Parmesan cheese. Pour 4 fl oz/120 ml of stock evenly over the baking dish, letting it seep down.
6   Bake, covered, at 400° F, 200° C, Gas Mark 6, for 30 minutes. Uncover and bake for 10–15 minutes more, until browned and bubbly and the stock has been absorbed.

BREAD AND CARAMELIZED ONION SOUFFLÉ

Serves 6–8

This is for people who find comfort in the gobs of melted cheese, the thick croûtons and the dark rich onions that are the glory of onion soup. Bread and onion soufflé is the soul of onion soup. It is, essentially, onion soup without the soup. Use the largest, sweetest Spanish onions that you can find. Leftovers reheat well in the microwave.

1 large garlic clove, split	6 tablespoons Parmesan cheese
4 large onions, peeled and trimmed	2 whole eggs plus 2 egg whites
1½ pts/900 ml stock	8 fl oz/240 ml skimmed milk
2 fl oz/60 ml dry vermouth	8 fl oz/240 ml stock
6 oz/180 g stale crusty French bread, cut into 1 inch/2.5 cm chunks	Salt and freshly ground pepper to taste

1   Preheat the oven to 350° F, 180° C, Gas Mark 4.
2   Choose a shallow round or oval gratin dish. Rub it thoroughly with the cut sides of the garlic clove. Discard the garlic.
3   Cut onions in half. Slice into thin half-moons. Combine onions

and 16 fl oz/480 ml of stock in a deep 10 inch/25 cm enamelled cast iron frying pan. Cover and bring to the boil. Reduce heat a bit and simmer briskly for 10 minutes.

4   Uncover the pot, raise the heat to medium, and cook, stirring occasionally, until the onions are amber brown. Pour in the vermouth and boil until the liquid cooks away, scraping the bottom of the pot with a wooden spoon all the while.

5   Toss the bread and onions together. Spread them in the gratin dish. Sprinkle on the grated cheese.

6   Beat the eggs and egg whites lightly together. Beat in the milk and salt and pepper. Pour the mixture evenly over the bread and cheese. Press the bread into the liquid with a spatula. Let stand for at least 1 hour. (The gratin may be covered and refrigerated overnight. On the next day bring it to room temperature before proceeding.)

7   Bake for 35–40 minutes, until set, puffed and golden. (A knife inserted near the centre will emerge clean.) If necessary, flash under the grill for a minute or two to brown the top. Serve at once.

♡ 🐻 ❄️   **BRAISED VEGETABLES**

Makes 2 pts/1200 ml

This lovely stew is wonderful when baby artichokes appear in the markets. When they are out of season, substitute tinned artichoke hearts. If you also substitute tinned peppers for the fresh ones, this becomes a fast dish indeed.

1 large onion, coarsely chopped	1 red and 1 yellow pepper,
6 fl oz/180 ml stock	peeled, seeded and cut into
2 tablespoons lemon juice	1/2 inch/1.25 cm strips
8 baby artichokes	Salt and freshly ground pepper to
1 small tin Italian tomatoes,	taste
drained and crushed	1 1/2 tablespoons chopped fresh oregano
3 stalks celery, sliced	1 1/2 tablespoons chopped fresh parsley
1 fennel bulb, trimmed and sliced	1 1/2 tablespoons chopped fresh
1/2 lb/240 g mushrooms, quartered	fennel leaves

1   Combine the onions, stock and lemon juice in a large, heavy, non-reactive frying pan. Cover and bring to the boil. Boil for 5 minutes. Uncover and simmer until the onions are amber brown and tender and the liquid is about gone.

2   Trim the artichokes: cut off stems, remove and discard tough outer leaves. Cut each in half. Stir the tomatoes and artichokes into the onion mixture. Simmer briskly, uncovered, for 10 minutes.

3   Stir in celery, fennel, mushrooms and peppers. Simmer un-
     covered, stirring occasionally, for about 30 minutes, until the
     vegetables are tender. If it gets too dry at any time, add a bit
     more stock.
4   Season with salt and pepper and stir in herbs.

⊕   Substitute tinned artichoke hearts for the fresh ones and
     tinned peppers for the fresh peppers.

Magical Mashed Spuds

There are few culinary therapies in the world as powerful as
mashed potatoes. I mean this quite seriously. Starchy, high-
carbohydrate foods are almost miraculous in their curative power.
Recent fascinating research suggests that certain foods cause con-
tentment and mood elevation by altering the amounts of key brain
chemicals in much the same way as drugs used to treat severe
depression. A chemical called serotonin must be present in the
brain in proper amounts, or downward mood swings occur. Drugs
in use for depression keep serotonin levels high by either retarding
the body's removal of serotonin or promoting its build-up. The
body makes serotonin from one of the components of dietary
proteins: the amino acid tryptophan. Under ordinary circumstances, tryptophan has to compete with other amino acids to get
into the brain. But when an individual ingests relatively more
carbohydrate than protein, tryptophan has less competition getting in. When more tryptophan gets into the brain, more serotonin
can be produced, and the individual feels calm and sleepy and
much less anxious.

Personally, I find that an evening meal of mashed potatoes
blankets me in a blissfully warm feeling of placid security. Don't
ever think that potatoes are fattening and should be avoided. A
medium potato contains about 90 fat-free Calories, and is bursting
with vitamins A, C, B1, B6, niacin, not to mention iron, potassium
and fibre. And a meal of potatoes leaves you feeling that you have
dined well and copiously. Why not have a mashed potato evening
every once in a while? Mound fluffy dollops of mashed spuds in a
shallow soup plate (use your best pottery, the potatoes will taste
even better). With a soup spoon, make a depression in the top
of the mound. Fill the depression with something wonderful:
Tomato-Broad Bean Ragoût, Mushroom Ragoût, 'Fried' Onions,
Savoury Peppers – whatever sounds most seductively delicious at
the time. Find a comfortable chair in a quiet corner, grab a large
spoon and eat slowly and happily.

'Nothing like mashed potatoes when you are feeling blue. Nothing like getting into bed with a bowl of hot mashed potatoes.'

Nora Ephron, *Heartburn*

♡ MASHED POTATOES

Because life's trials and tribulations are eased by generous and frequent helpings of mashed spuds, quick methods of preparing them are desparately needed. Here are two suggestions.

1 Microwave ⊠ ⏱

Choose large (½ lb/225 g each) baking potatoes. Prick them several times with a fork or thin skewer. Timing is as follows:

1 potato   – 7 minutes
2 potatoes – 11 minutes
3 potatoes – 16 minutes
4 potatoes – 20 minutes

When the time is up, use an oven glove to remove each potato from the oven. Squeeze the potato gently, then strip off the skin. Mash the potatoes with an old-fashioned masher, then – with an electric beater – beat in fromage frais, salt and freshly ground pepper.

2 Instant ⏱

I used to sneer at instant mashed potatoes, in fact I used to insist that you might as well eat the box and throw away the potatoes. I've changed my tune, but keep a few rules in mind.

1   Don't use the kind of instant potatoes that are made up of little pellets.

2   Don't use mashed potatoes that list salt, fat, or flavourings in the ingredients. (As of this writing, I find Waitrose brand instant potatoes to be excellent.)

3   Follow directions on the box as to amount of water. Ignore exhortations about knobs of butter or margarine. When the potatoes and water have been thoroughly mixed, beat in fromage frais until the potatoes are beautifully creamy. (I add almost a full carton of fromage frais for each large sachet of potatoes.) Season with salt and pepper.

PIPERADE POTATOES

Serves 6

Mashed potatoes mixed with herbed, sautéed vegetables make a lovely main dish, for nights when you want a meatless supper, but it's also good as an accompaniment to meat or poultry. When you are in a hurry, microwave your potatoes and use tinned peppers (see page 24), but Piperade Potatoes are at their best when prepared as the recipe is written.

---

3 large onions, cut in half and sliced into paper-thin half-moons
4 fl oz/120 ml stock
3 large cloves garlic, crushed
3 large bell peppers, cut in half lengthwise, sliced and peeled into thin strips (use 1 red, 1 green, 1 yellow if possible)
1 large tin (1 lb 12 oz/840 g) tomatoes, well drained, seeded and sliced into strips

Salt and freshly ground pepper to taste
¼ teaspoon dried oregano, crumbled
¼ teaspoon dried basil, crumbled
4 fl oz/120 ml chopped fresh parsley
4 large baking potatoes, baked
2 fl oz/60 ml grated Parmesan cheese

---

1   Combine the onions in 4 fl oz/120 ml stock in a wide, heavy, non-reactive frying pan. Cover and bring to the boil. Cook for 3–4 minutes. Uncover, turn heat down. Simmer briskly until onions are tender and amber brown. Use a splash more stock if needed to scrape up the browned bits on the bottom of the pan.
2   Add the garlic and peppers. Cook, stirring occasionally, until the peppers are tender. Stir in the tomatoes, dried herbs and parsley. Simmer, uncovered, until thick and saucy. Season to taste.
3   Preheat the oven to 400° F, 200° C, Gas Mark 6.
4   Perforate the potatoes and squeeze so the flesh surges up. Scoop into a bowl, mash well. Beat in the vegetable mixture. Taste and adjust seasoning. Spread into a shallow 9 in × 13 in/23 cm × 33 cm baking dish. Sprinkle evenly with cheese. (Save the potato skins for a special treat, see below.) Bake uncovered for ½ hour, until browned and bubbly.

♡ Omit cheese.

⧖ ⊕ Microwave the potatoes and use tinned peppers.

Potato skins make a delectable snack. Cut them into strips and arrange on the grill tray. Sprinkle with Parmesan cheese and freshly ground pepper. Grill for approximately 2 minutes, until the cheese is melted and the potato skins are crispy. Serve hot. Or save the skins for Potato Nachos (see page 43).

♡ Omit cheese; grill for 1–1½ minutes.

HUNGARIAN POTATO RAGOÛT

Makes 2 pts/1200 ml

Szekely goulash, that star of all Hungarian pork stews, works beautifully and deliciously with potatoes taking the place of the pork. Vegetarians should leave out the small amount of optional lean bacon, added at the end. If you wish, garnish each serving with a dollop of fromage frais. This is the sort of hearty cookery that comforts the deep corners of the soul.

---

1 jar sauerkraut
3 medium onions, halved and sliced
  into thin half-moons
3 cloves garlic, crushed
¼ teaspoon thyme
Approximately 12 fl oz/360 ml
  stock
2 fl oz/60 ml dry white vermouth
1½ tablespoons Hungarian sweet
  paprika or paprika paste

Pinch or two of cayenne pepper
1 tablespoon caraway seeds
1 tin (14 oz/420 g) chopped
  tomatoes
2 large all-purpose potatoes, halved
  lengthwise and cut into
  ½ inch/1.25 cm chunks
Salt and freshly ground pepper to
  taste
¼ lb/120 g lean, thin sliced bacon,
  chopped (optional)

---

1   Preheat the oven to 350° F, 180° C, Gas Mark 4.
2   Drain sauerkraut in a colander. Rinse well under cold water. Drain again and squeeze as dry as possible. Set aside.
3   Combine the onions, garlic, thyme, 4 fl oz/120 ml stock and the vermouth in a heavy non-reactive frying pan. Cover and simmer for 10 minutes. Uncover and cook over a moderate heat, stirring frequently, until the liquid is almost gone and the onions are browned.
4   Off the heat, stir in the paprika, cayenne pepper and caraway seeds. Stir for a few moments, until the onions are well coated with the paprika and it has lost its raw taste.
5   Toss in the tomatoes, the sauerkraut and the potatoes. Combine everything well. Dump the mixture into a non-reactive casserole. Season with salt and pepper and pour in stock

to just barely cover the contents. Cover closely and bake for 1 hour.

6   Meanwhile, if you are using the bacon, gently sauté it, stirring, for a minute or so, in a non-stick frying pan. After the potatoes have cooked for 1 hour, scrape the bacon mixture into the casserole and gently stir in. Cover and bake for an additional ½ hour, or until the potatoes are tender.

♡   Omit bacon.

❋ POTATO STEFADO

Makes 3½ pts/2100 ml

A vegetarian version of the fragrant Greek beef stew on page 71.

¾ lb/360 g mushrooms, halved or quartered, depending on size	4 fl oz/120 ml chopped fresh parsley
3 large all-purpose potatoes, halved lengthwise and cut into 1½ inch/1.25 cm chunks	1 bay leaf
	1 teaspoon dried oregano
	1 teaspoon ground cinnamon
8 shallots, cut into quarters or eighths, depending on size	1 teaspoon ground cumin
	2 fl oz/60 ml red wine vinegar
4 cloves garlic, crushed	Approximately 8 fl oz/240 ml stock
1 large cauliflower, trimmed and broken into large florets	
	Garnish
2 rounded tablespoons tomato paste	Crumbled medium-fat feta cheese
Salt and freshly ground pepper to taste	Chopped parsley

1   Preheat oven to 350° F, 180° C, Gas Mark 4.
2   Combine all ingredients, except garnishes, in a non-reactive casserole that works on top of the stove as well as in the oven. Bring to the boil.
3   Cover tightly. Bake for 1–1¼ hours.
4   Garnish each serving with some feta and parsley.

♡   Omit the feta cheese.

♡ ⊕ ❋ POTATO-PEPPER STEW

Makes 3½ pts/2100 ml

Unsophisticated, filling and delicious. A huge bowlful is just the ticket at the end of a long day; you'll nourish both body and soul. If you wish, top each serving with a dollop of fromage frais.

3 large onions, coarsely chopped
3 cloves garlic, crushed
1 stalk celery, cut in half lengthwise
  and sliced
1 carrot, peeled and diced
Approximately 1½ pts/900 ml stock
6 medium 'all-purpose' (Willja
  work well) potatoes, unpeeled,
  diced into 1 inch/2.5 cm pieces

6 large red and/or yellow peppers,
  peeled and diced into 1 inch/2.5
  cm pieces
1 tin (14 oz/420 g) chopped Italian
  tomatoes
3 tablespoons chopped parsley
3 tablespoons chopped fresh basil
¼ teaspoon crushed dried chillies
  (or to taste)
Salt and pepper to taste

1   Combine onions, garlic, celery, carrot and 8 fl oz/240 ml of
     stock in a heavy, wide pot. Cover and boil for 5–10 minutes
     until tender and beginning to brown and stick to the pan.
     Uncover, stir and cook over moderate heat, adding a splash of
     stock as needed, and scraping up the browned bits, until the
     onions are amber brown, meltingly tender and syrupy.
2   Add the potatoes and peppers and stir until very well com-
     bined. Stir in all remaining ingredients. Pour in enough stock
     to almost cover the contents of the pot. Simmer, partially
     covered, stirring occasionally, until the potatoes are tender,
     about 30 minutes.

     # POTATO CHILLI

Makes 2 pts/1200 ml

Chilli con Patate is even better than Chilli con Carne; potatoes soak
up seasonings so beautifully. This is the sort of good home cooking
you'll find yourself making over and over again.

Approximately 12 fl oz/360 ml
  chicken or vegetable stock
3 large onions, halved and sliced
  into thin half-moons
2 cloves garlic, minced
1 teaspoon crumbled dried oregano
2 tablespoons chilli powder
1 teaspoon ground cumin
Cayenne pepper to taste

3 rounded tablespoons tomato paste
3 large all-purpose potatoes, halved
  and cut into 1½ inch/4 cm
  chunks
Salt and freshly ground pepper to
  taste
Grated Parmesan cheese
Fromage frais
Pepper Salad (recipe follows)

1   Preheat the oven to 350° F, 180° C, Gas Mark 4.
2   Combine 4 fl oz/120 ml of the stock with the onions and garlic
     in a heavy frying pan. Cover and simmer briskly for 10
     minutes.
3   Uncover and cook for 5–7 minutes, or until the onions are

tender and browned and the liquid has cooked away. Stir in the oregano and spices. Stir over lowest heat until the onions are well coated with the spices, then blend in the tomato paste.

4   Toss the potatoes in the onion mixture. Season with salt and pepper. Pour in the remaining stock, and bring to a simmer, stirring. Scrape the mixture into a casserole. Cover and bake for 1–1¼ hours, or until the potatoes are tender and the sauce is very thick and rich. (This reheats well but you may have to add more stock.)

5   Serve in shallow soup bowls. Top each serving with a sprinkling of cheese, a dollop of fromage frais and a spoonful of Pepper Salad. Serve kidney beans on the side, if desired.

Pepper Salad

1 large green pepper, peeled and diced	1 tablespoon chopped fresh parsley
	½ tablespoon chopped fresh coriander
1 large red pepper, peeled and diced	Juice of 1 lime
1 large yellow pepper, peeled and diced	Salt to taste
3 thin spring onions, sliced	½ teaspoon sugar

Toss all the ingredients together in a bowl at least ½ hour before serving.

♡ Omit Parmesan cheese.

TURNIP-POTATO RATATOUILLE

Makes 2½ pts/1500 ml

Turnips and potatoes take the place of the traditional courgettes and aubergines in this main dish ratatouille.

2 medium onions, cut in half and sliced into paper-thin half-moons	3 ripe tomatoes, peeled, seeded, juiced and chopped (or substitute tinned)
6 fl oz/180 ml stock	
1 small red pepper, peeled and sliced	Salt and freshly ground pepper to taste
1 small yellow pepper, peeled and sliced	3 tablespoons shredded fresh basil or ¼ teaspoon crumbled dried basil
1 small green pepper, peeled and sliced	3 tablespoons chopped fresh parsley
3 cloves garlic, crushed	3 small waxy potatoes, coarsely diced
3 small turnips, peeled and coarsely diced	4 fl oz/120 ml grated Parmesan cheese

1   Combine the onions and 4 fl oz/120 ml stock in a frying pan.
    Cover and bring to the boil. Boil for 3–4 minutes.
2   Uncover and turn the heat down a bit. Simmer briskly, stir-
    ring, until the onions are tender and amber brown. Pour in a
    splash of additional stock and boil, stirring and scraping the
    browned bits on the bottom of the pan. Stir in the peppers and
    the garlic. Cook for a few minutes until the peppers lose their
    crispness.
3   Stir in turnips, tomatoes, seasonings and herbs. Cover and
    simmer very gently for 10 minutes. Add the potatoes, cover
    and simmer until the turnips and potatoes are tender. Spread
    the mixture in a gratin pan and sprinkle the surface with the
    cheese. At this point the dish may be refrigerated until serving
    time, for a day or two if necessary. In fact the flavour will
    improve. Bring to room temperature before proceeding.
4   Preheat the oven to 350° F, 180° C, Gas Mark 4. Bake the
    ratatouille, uncovered, until bubbling and lightly browned on
    top, about 20 minutes.

♡   Omit Parmesan cheese.

 # LAYERED POLENTA AND AUBERGINE

Serves 6

Polenta is coarse cornmeal; when added to boiling liquid and
stirred over a modest flame, it cooks into a thick yellow corn
porridge, the basis of countless comforting supper possibilities.
Quick-cooking polenta, available in boxes from Italian delicatessens and many speciality food shops, cooks in 5 minutes. If you
spoon the hot cooked polenta into a loaf tin, or into clean empty
tins, and set it aside while you make a quick sauce, the polenta will
be ready to be unmoulded, sliced and grilled (or simmered in the
sauce) by the time the sauce is done. To me, an evening meal of
polenta with a hearty sauce or ragoût is one of the happiest of
culinary occasions. I put it right up there with mashed potato
evenings.

34 fl oz/1020 ml stock or salted water

8 fl oz/240 ml quick-cooking polenta (coarse maize meal)

1 large onion, coarsely chopped

1 red or yellow pepper, peeled and coarsely chopped

2 cloves garlic, crushed

½ teaspoon dried basil

4 fl oz/120 ml stock

4 fl oz/120 ml dry red wine

2 tins (12 oz/360 g each) chopped tomatoes

4–6 ripe tomatoes, peeled and seeded

1 piece Parmesan rind

2–3 tablespoons tomato paste

4 tablespoons chopped fresh parsley

2 medium aubergines

6 tablespoons grated Parmesan cheese

1   Bring 34 fl oz/1020 ml of stock or salted water to the boil. With a wire whisk, whisk in the polenta. (Whisk well so that the mixture does not form lumps.) Bring to the boil, immediately lower the heat, and cook on low heat, stirring (switch to a wooden spoon), for about 5 minutes until smooth and very thick. As it cooks, taste for seasonings and add salt if needed. Be careful it does not scorch. Pack into two clean round tins (the tins from the chopped tomatoes will do), cover with cling film and refrigerate.

2   Combine onion, pepper, garlic, basil, stock and wine. Cover and bring to the boil. Reduce heat and simmer for about 10 minutes. Uncover and continue cooking until vegetables are tender and the liquid is about gone. Stir in the tomatoes and Parmesan rind. Simmer for 15–20 minutes. Stir in tomato paste and parsley. Simmer for 5 minutes more. Season with salt and pepper. Set aside.

3   Pierce each aubergine several times with a thin skewer or fork. Put a paper towel on your microwave carousel and place aubergines on it. Microwave on high for 3 minutes, turning them once, after 1½ minutes. Remove from the oven and let stand for 3 minutes.

4   Slice the aubergine (unpeeled) into ½ inch/1.25 cm slices. Push or shake the polenta out of the tin (it will come out in a lovely, compact cylinder). The top of each cylinder will be crusty; take a thin slice off the top and discard. Slice the remainder approximately ½ inch/1.25 cm thick. Overlap alternating slices of polenta and aubergine in a shallow baking dish. Spread the sauce over them and sprinkle with the grated cheese. Bake at 350° F, 180° C, Gas Mark 4, for 30 minutes, or until hot and bubbly.

♡ Omit Parmesan cheese.

Variation I: Grilled Polenta with Herbed Onions or Intense Mushroom Ragoût ♡ ⏱

Polenta (see recipe above, step 1)
Herbed Onions (see page 117) or
Intense Mushroom Ragoût (see
page 118)

---

1   Line the grill tray with foil, shiny side out. Preheat the grill to its highest point.
2   In a saucepan, heat the Herbed Onions or Intense Mushroom Ragoût.
3   Shake the polenta out of the tins and slice. Place the polenta slices in a single layer on a non-stick baking sheet. Grill 6 inches/15 cm from the heat for approximately 6 minutes, until beginning to brown on top.
4   Mound the Herbed Onions or Intense Mushroom Ragoût on a serving dish. With a fish slice, carefully lift the polenta slices off the baking sheet. Overlap them around the onions or mushrooms and serve at once.

Variation II: Grilled Polenta with Tomato-Broad Bean Ragoût ⏱

Polenta (see main recipe, step 1)   *Thinly sliced Italian Mozzarella*
Tomato-Broad Bean Ragoût (see   *cheese*
page 117)   *Freshly ground pepper to taste*

---

1   Preheat the grill to its highest point.
2   Shake the polenta out of the tins. Slice the polenta and arrange in one layer on a non-stick baking sheet. Grill, 6 inches/15 cm from the heat, for approximately 6 minutes, until beginning to brown on top.
3   Spoon sauce generously over the polenta rounds. Top each round with a slice of Mozzarella cheese. Sprinkle generously with freshly ground pepper. Grill, 3 inches/8 cm from the heat, for 3–4 minutes or until the cheese is melted, bubbly and speckled with brown. Lift slices off the sheet with a fish slice and place on plates. Or the polenta rounds can be placed in a baking dish in one layer. Spread the sauce over the polenta, and lay cheese slices over the top. Grill until bubbly and lightly browned. Serve from the baking dish.

♡   Omit cheese.

TOMATO-BROAD BEAN RAGOÛT

Makes 3½–4 pts/2100–2400 ml

Tomato-broad bean ragoût can be eaten from a bowl as a thick soup, or it can accompany polenta or mashed potatoes. You may want to try it tossed with penne (pasta quills) as well.

---

2 large tins Italian plum tomatoes
Pinch or two dried crushed chillies
   (optional)
1 large tin (14 oz/420 g) pimientos
   (red peppers)
1 piece Parmesan cheese rind

Handful coarsely chopped sun-dried
   tomatoes (optional)
1 tin (14 oz/420 g) broad beans
Freshly ground pepper to taste
2–3 tablespoons tomato paste
Chopped fresh parsley

---

1   Dump the plum tomatoes, juice and all, into a non-reactive saucepan. With a potato masher, roughly crush them. Sprinkle in the chillies.

2   Drain the liquid from the pimiento tin. With a pair of kitchen scissors, roughly chop up the pimientos, right in the tin. Dump them in with the tomatoes. Add the Parmesan rind and the sun-dried tomatoes, if you are using them. Bring to the boil.

3   Reduce heat and simmer for about 10 minutes. Add the drained broad beans and pepper and simmer for 10 minutes more. Stir in the tomato paste and simmer for 5–10 minutes more, or until thick. Taste, and add a pinch of sugar if it seems too acidic. If you have some fresh parsley, stir in a handful of chopped leaves. Serve with Mashed Potatoes (page 108), jacket potatoes, Polenta (page 114), or pasta.

HERBED ONIONS FOR POLENTA

Makes 1½ pts/900 ml

Braised onions with parsley, rosemary, fennel and a touch of red wine vinegar.

---

2 large cloves garlic, peeled
¼ pt/150 ml fresh parsley
½ tablespoon rosemary leaves
½ teaspoon fennel seeds (optional)
4 large Spanish onions, peeled, cut
   in half and sliced into thin
   half-moons

12 fl oz/360 ml stock
2 tablespoons red wine vinegar
1 tablespoon tomato paste
3–4 fl oz/90–120 ml stock
Salt and freshly ground pepper to
   taste

---

1   Chop together the garlic, parsley, rosemary and optional
     fennel seeds. Set aside.
2   Combine the onions and 12 fl oz/360 ml stock in a deep, heavy,
     non-reactive frying pan that can be covered. Cover and bring
     to the boil. Boil for about 5–7 minutes. Uncover. Continue to
     cook, stirring occasionally, until the liquid is almost gone and
     the onions are beginning to brown and stick to the pan.
     Continue cooking for a moment or two. Pour in a splash of
     stock, and stir and scrape up the browned bits with a wooden
     spoon.
3   When the onions are amber brown and meltingly tender, stir
     in the garlic mixture. Stir together the wine vinegar, tomato
     paste and 3–4 fl oz/90–120 ml stock. Stir into the onions.
     Simmer, uncovered, for 5–10 minutes. Season to taste.

 ## INTENSE MUSHROOM
        RAGOÛT

Makes 2 pts/1200 ml

Dried mushrooms and their soaking juices add a new dimension to
mushroom ragoût.

2 lb/960 g of mixed fresh mushrooms (look for fresh shiitake, chestnut and oyster mushrooms in addition to the ordinary cultivated ones; trim the tough stems from shiitakes before using them)	*Freshly ground pepper to taste*
	Dash of teriyaki sauce
	1 fl oz/30 ml medium sherry
	2 fl oz/60 ml each stock and mushroom soaking water (see below)
1 oz/30 g Reconstituted Dried Mushrooms (see below)	*1 fl oz/30 ml balsamic vinegar*

1   Clean fresh mushrooms well, cut into quarters or eighths
     (depending on size) and combine with Reconstituted Dried
     Mushrooms, seasonings and liquids in a large, heavy, non-
     reactive frying pan.
2   Simmer, stirring occasionally. The mushrooms will exude a
     good deal of liquid. Continue cooking until the liquid is greatly
     reduced.
3   Cook, stirring, until the mushrooms are tender, and 'frying' in
     their syrupy sauce. Taste and correct seasonings.

Reconstituted Dried Mushrooms

1 oz/30 g dried cèpes/porcini

Rinse the dried mushrooms well under cold running water. Soak in hot water to cover generously for 1 hour. Strain the water through a double cheesecloth-lined sieve or a coffee filter, and reserve. Rinse the mushrooms under cold running water. Trim off and discard any tough stems. Chop the mushrooms coarsely. Use some of the filtered soaking water to cook the ragoût. Save the remainder for soups and sauce.

♡ 🧸 ⏲   **VEGETABLE GUMBO**

Makes 5 pts/3000 ml

A thick, inelegant, extremely savoury vegetable stew with the consistency of a gumbo. Traditionally, gumbos are thickened with an oily dark roux, or with filé powder (powdered sassafras leaves), or both; this one gets its texture from baked aubergine and garlic. It is basically a pantry recipe, utilizing several excellent tinned and frozen products. Make it even quicker and more convenient to prepare by baking the aubergine and garlic in the microwave and substituting tinned pimientos for the fresh peppers. This concoction freezes very well.

2 large Spanish onions, cut in half and sliced into thin half-moons	3 tins (14 oz/420 g each) chopped tomatoes
10 fl oz/300 ml stock	Purée from 1 large head Baked Garlic (see page 17)
¼ pt/150 ml dry red wine	Chopped pulp from 2 Baked Aubergines (see page 21)
2 red peppers, sliced into strips and peeled	Salt and pepper to taste
2 yellow peppers, sliced into strips and peeled	4 rounded tablespoons tomato paste
1 teaspoon (or to taste) crushed dried chillies	1 tin artichoke hearts, drained and quartered
1 large packet (2 lb/960 g) frozen sweetcorn kernels, partially thawed	4–5 tablespoons chopped fresh parsley
1 large packet (2 lb/960 g) frozen button Brussels sprouts, partially thawed	

1   Combine the onions and the stock in a large saucepan. Cover and bring to the boil. Uncover. Boil for approximately

119

5 minutes, until most of the liquid has cooked away. Reduce heat and simmer until just about dry and beginning to stick a little bit.

2   Uncover and lower the heat. Toss and stir constantly with a wooden spoon until you smell a lovely, toasty, oniony aroma and the bottom of the pan is beginning to brown just a bit. Pour in the wine and turn the heat up again. Stir with the wooden spoon, scraping up all the browned bits. When the liquid is gone, the onions should be meltingly tender and amber-coloured.

3   Stir in the peppers, crushed chillies, corn, sprouts, tomatoes, garlic, aubergine, salt and pepper. Simmer, uncovered, for 15 minutes.

4   Stir in the tomato paste and artichoke hearts. Simmer, uncovered, for 10–15 minutes longer. Stir in the parsley and adjust seasonings.

⊠ ⏱ Bake the aubergine and garlic in the microwave, and use tinned peppers.

Side Dishes and Sauces

'Your exploration of food should be governed by infinite curiosity. Fling open the gastronomic gates . . .'

Dana Kaye, *The Travelling Woman*

GREEN BEAN SOUFFLÉ

Serves 6

This is an easy soufflé: impressive and unusual as a first course, or as an accompaniment to meat or poultry.

---

1 lb/480 g frozen green beans	2 fl oz/60 ml dry vermouth
5 shallots or onions, halved and thinly sliced	6 fl oz/180 ml rich stock
1 large clove garlic, minced	Salt and freshly ground pepper to taste
1 teaspoon dried basil	4 oz/120 g quark
1 teaspoon sweet Hungarian paprika or paprika paste	2 tablespoons Parmesan cheese
Pinch or two of cayenne pepper	8 egg whites, at room temperature
	Pinch of cream of tartar

---

1   Steam the green beans until very tender. Set aside.
2   Combine shallots, garlic, basil, paprika, cayenne pepper, vermouth and 2 fl oz/60 ml of stock in a small frying pan. Boil, stirring occasionally, until the mixture is almost dry. Set aside.
3   Combine the beans, shallot infusion, remaining stock and quark in the container of a liquidizer, and purée.
4   Rub the purée through a sieve into saucepan. Heat it very gently. Taste and adjust seasonings. (It should be quite peppery.) Cool.
5   Stir Parmesan cheese into the cooled mixture.
6   Beat egg whites in an electric mixer on slow speed. Add pinch of cream of tartar and beat on highest speed until whites hold firm peaks.
7   Gently fold the whites into the green bean mixture.
8   Spoon the green bean mixture into a soufflé dish. Cook on the middle shelf of the oven for 40 minutes, until puffed and firm. (Remove the rack above before baking.) Serve at once.

CAULIFLOWER AND PEPPERS

Serves 4

The ivory-white cauliflower pieces, studded with crimson pepper strips, look so pretty, and the tastes and textures of the two vegetables play against each other very well.

---

1 large cauliflower, trimmed and separated into florets	6 fl oz/180 ml stock
2 large red peppers, seeded, ribbed and cut into their natural sections	1 clove garlic, minced
	1/2 teaspoon cumin seeds
	Salt and freshly ground pepper to taste

---

1   Steam the cauliflower over boiling water, until partially
     cooked, about 3 minutes. Refresh under cold water and set
     aside.
2   With a swivel-bladed vegetable peeler, peel each pepper
     piece. Cut the peppers into strips about ½ inch/1.25 cm wide.
3   Heat half the stock in a heavy frying pan. When it begins to
     bubble, stir in the garlic and peppers. Stir and toss with two
     wooden spoons until the peppers are almost crisp tender and
     the liquid is almost gone. Lower heat and let the peppers 'fry'
     gently in their own juices as you stir them. When they are very
     tender, stir in the cauliflower.
4   Sprinkle in the cumin and stir well. Pour in the remaining
     stock. Cover and simmer until the cauliflower is tender but not
     mushy. Season to taste.

🕐   Substitute tinned peppers for the fresh ones.

❄   # VEGETABLE STUFFED
    # PEPPERS

Makes 12 pieces

Don't grumble about the extra work of peeling the peppers. When
peeled, their delicious juices mingle with the stock and tomato
paste to form a splendid sauce. And the texture of the peeled
peppers is very special.

Several dashes soy sauce	*Salt and freshly ground pepper to*
4 fl oz/120 ml stock	*taste*
2 fl oz/60 ml sherry	*¼ teaspoon grated nutmeg*
2 cloves garlic, crushed	*6 large red or yellow peppers,*
8 fl oz/240 ml coarsely grated,	*halved lengthwise, seeded and*
peeled raw carrot	*peeled with a swivel-bladed*
8 fl oz/240 ml coarsely grated,	*peeler, or in the microwave (see*
peeled white turnip	*page 24)*
4 fl oz/120 ml coarsely grated onion	*4 tablespoons grated Parmesan*
4 fl oz/120 ml coarsely grated,	*cheese*
unpeeled all-purpose potato	*8 fl oz/240 ml stock*
4 fl oz/120 ml pine nuts	*2 fl oz/60 ml tomato paste*
4 fl oz/120 ml raisins, soaked in	
4 fl oz/120 ml dry sherry for	
15 minutes	

1   Preheat oven to 350° F, 180° C, Gas Mark 4.
2   Heat soy sauce, stock and sherry in a large frying pan. Add
     vegetables and toss until tender but not at all mushy, and the
     liquid is almost gone.

3   Stir in nuts, drained raisins, salt, pepper and nutmeg. Set aside.
4   Arrange the peppers, peeled side down, in one or two baking dishes. Fill each half with an equal amount of vegetable mixture. Sprinkle each with 1 teaspoon Parmesan cheese.
5   Whisk together the remaining ingredients. Pour around the peppers. Cover the dish with foil and bake for 1 hour.

 Omit pine nuts and Parmesan cheese
Omit pine nuts, Parmesan cheese and raisins.

SAVOURY PEPPERS

Makes 2 pts/1200 ml

This is a sumptuous Slim Cuisine stir-'fry'. Turn it into a pretty first course by tossing in some tiny cooked peeled prawns at the very end. Add a teaspoon of chopped drained capers as well.

6–8 red peppers	2 fl oz/60 ml sherry
4–5 cloves garlic, peeled and coarsely diced	Splash of balsamic vinegar (optional)
4 fl oz/120 ml vegetable stock	Freshly ground pepper to taste

1   Stem and seed peppers, cut into ½ inch/1.25 cm wide strips. Peel each strip with a swivel-bladed vegetable peeler.
2   Combine peppers and remaining ingredients in a heavy, non-reactive frying pan. Bring to a boil. Cook, stirring occasionally, until the peppers are tender and the liquid is greatly reduced. Continue to stir and cook – the peppers and garlic chunks will be 'frying' in their own juices – until the peppers are in a thick, syrupy, scant sauce. Serve at once, or cool for a later time.

BRAISED CARROTS

Carrots braised in fresh citrus juices until tender make a good addition to Sunday lunch or a holiday dinner.

Large carrots, peeled and cut in half lengthwise	1 inch/2.5 cm piece each lemon zest and orange zest
Stock	2–3 large cloves garlic, peeled and halved
Juice of 1 large orange	
Juice of ½ large lemon	Salt and freshly ground pepper to taste

1   Preheat oven to 400° F, 200° C, Gas Mark 6.
2   Arrange carrots, in one layer, in a shallow baking dish. Pour in
     stock to a depth of a little less than ½ inch/1.25 cm. Pour the
     juices over the carrots and scatter in the lemon and orange zest
     and the garlic. Season lightly with salt and generously with
     freshly ground pepper. Cover the dish with foil, shiny side in.
3   Bake for 45 minutes. Uncover and bake for 15 minutes more.
     By then the carrots should be tender, and the liquid gone.
     Serve at once, or refrigerate or freeze until needed. Reheat in
     the microwave or conventional oven. Add a bit of stock first.

♡ ❄ BRAISED SHALLOTS

Makes 1 pt/600 ml

These shallots are meant to be served as a chutney or a relish. They
go very well with Grilled Goose Skirt Steak (page 67) or Hamburgers (*Slim Cuisine I*).

---

2 tablespoons golden raisins	*Grated zest of ½ lemon*
8 fl oz/240 ml dry red wine	*Salt and freshly ground pepper*
12 fl oz/360 ml stock	*Juice of ½ lemon (to taste)*
1½ lb/720 g shallots, peeled and	
* halved (substitute thinly sliced*	
* onions when shallots are*	
* unavailable)*	

---

1   Combine the raisins and wine in a small bowl. Set aside.
2   Pour 4 fl oz/120 ml stock into a heavy non-reactive frying pan.
     Add shallots. Cook over medium heat, shaking the pan fre-
     quently, until the shallots are lightly browned and the stock
     has almost cooked away.
3   Add the remaining stock, the wine, raisins, lemon zest and
     salt and pepper. Cook, partially covered, for 30 minutes, until
     the shallots are very tender. Squeeze in the lemon juice. Serve
     cold.

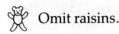 Omit raisins.

♡ 🧸 🕐 ❄ SAUTÉED SPRING ONIONS

Imagine trying to cook without onions! The mind boggles. Slim,
elegant spring onions are usually sliced and used as a garnish or
salad ingredient, but they make a delectable vegetable, cooked
whole, in quantity. Make plenty of these, they are moreish, to say
the least.

Thin spring onions
Stock

1   Trim the onions of their 'beard' and of all but 1–2 inches/ 2.5–5 cm of their green.
2   Heat ¼ inch/0.6 cm of stock in a heavy, wide frying pan. Arrange the spring onions in the pan in one layer. Cook over high heat, turning the onions occasionally with tongs, until the onions are tender and bathed in a syrupy glaze. Serve at once.

Variation: Gratin of Spring Onions

Place the sautéed spring onions in a shallow baking dish and, with a rubber spatula, scrape the glaze over them. The onions should be lying in one direction, and in one layer. Sprinkle with a small amount of Parmesan cheese and drizzle with a small amount of stock. Bake at 350° F, 180° C, Gas Mark 5, until heated through and the cheese has melted, 15–20 minutes.

A Vegetable Selection

Lavishness is one of the best aspects of Slim Cuisine. With the fat density gone, Calories are low, and some foods can be eaten in vast quantities with no fear of bulging out of one's clothes the next day. Vegetables fall into this category. With no butter, oil, or margarine used in their preparation, vegetables are extremely low in Calories yet they are high in vitamins, minerals and fibre. Not only *can* you eat large quantities, you *should*. Large and frequent helpings of vegetables are important to your nutritional well-being. Slim Cuisine techniques make them a pleasure to eat; your psycho-logical well-being will benefit as well.

For a special dinner party, serve Braised Brisket of Beef (page 68) and a vast selection of vegetables. Include Sautéed Mushrooms, 'Fried' Onions, Sautéed Spring Onions or Braised Leeks, Stir-'Fried' Peppers or Savoury Peppers, Stir-'Fried' Courgettes (*Slim Cuisine I*) or Baked Courgettes, Spicy Sprouts, Braised Fennel (*Slim Cuisine I*) and Roast Potatoes. These veg-etables, arranged on a large plate, make a wonderfully tempting edible mosaic; one that guests will dig into with a feeling of delighted exhilaration. *All* the vegetables on the plate can be prepared ahead of time, some as early as two days ahead. The onions, peppers and mushrooms may be prepared weeks ahead and frozen.

126

'One of the greatest luxuries in dining is to be able to command plenty of good vegetables well served up.'

Thomas Walker, *The Art of Dining*

✳ BRAISED LEEKS

Makes 12 pieces

12 leeks	*4 fl oz/120 ml stock*
Freshly ground pepper	*3 tablespoons Parmesan cheese*

1   Preheat oven to 350° F, 180° C, Gas Mark 4.
2   Trim off 'beard' and all but ¼ inch/0.6 cm of green portion of leeks. (Save greens for stock.) Clean the leeks well. Arrange them in one layer in a baking dish and pour the stock over them. Sprinkle with the cheese and pepper.
3   Bake uncovered for 30–45 minutes, turning the leeks once during this time. They are done when they are tender, and the stock has cooked down to a glaze.

   Omit cheese.

BAKED COURGETTES, ITALIAN STYLE

Makes 1½ pts/900 ml

Courgettes, zucchini, green summer squash; whatever you call them, they are wonderful simmered in a thick tomato sauce. If you are feeling self-indulgent, add a handful of sun-dried tomatoes.

1 large onion, coarsely chopped	*2 tins (14 oz/420 g each) chopped*
1–2 large cloves garlic, coarsely	*Italian tomatoes*
chopped	*1 piece Parmesan rind*
6 fl oz/180 ml dry red wine	*3 tablespoons tomato paste*
6 fl oz/180 ml stock	*8 medium courgettes, sliced*
Handful sun-dried tomatoes,	*½ inch/1.25 cm thick*
chopped (optional)	*4 fl oz/120 ml chopped fresh parsley*
Generous pinch oregano	*A scattering of shredded fresh basil*
Salt and freshly ground pepper to	*leaves*
taste	

1   Combine onions, garlic, wine, stock, sun-dried tomatoes and oregano in a heavy non-reactive frying pan. Cover and bring

to the boil. Reduce heat and simmer briskly until almost all the liquid has been evaporated. Uncover, and cook gently, letting the onions and tomatoes 'fry' in their own juices. Season to taste.

2   Stir in the chopped tomatoes, Parmesan rind, salt and pepper. Simmer, partially covered, for 15 minutes. Stir in the tomato paste and simmer for 5 minutes more. Taste and adjust seasonings. Discard the Parmesan rind.

3   Stir in courgettes. Bake, uncovered, at 350° F, 180° C, Gas Mark 4, for 30–40 minutes, until the courgettes are tender. Stir occasionally during this time. Garnish with herbs and serve.

♡ 🧸 ⏰   **SPICY SPROUTS**

Makes 2 pts/1200 ml sprouts

Brown rice wine vinegar, soy sauce, and chilli and garlic paste are available in most supermarkets. If you don't want to gussy up your sprouts with such tastes, leave them out by all means.

---

1 large bag (2 lb/960 g) frozen baby Brussels sprouts	1 teaspoon brown rice wine vinegar
12 fl oz/360 ml stock	½ teaspoon soy sauce
Freshly ground pepper and crushed dried chilli to taste	½ teaspoon chilli and garlic paste

---

1   Place the still-frozen sprouts, stock and peppers in a wide, heavy, non-reactive frying pan. Cover and cook over high heat until the stock comes to the boil.

2   Uncover and cook, stirring, until the sprouts are thawed and just barely warm. They should still be crunchy.

3   Drain well and return liquid to the pan. Stir in remaining ingredients. Boil rapidly until greatly reduced.

4   Return sprouts to pan. Stir and cook gently until the sprouts are tender, hot and glazed. Taste and adjust seasonings.

This may be prepared a few days ahead of time and stored in the refrigerator. The sprouts are as delicious cold as hot.

♡ 🧸 ❄   **WHIPPED SWEDES**

Makes 2¼ pts/1110 ml

I *love* swedes; I even loved them back home in the States where they are known as rutabagas – an ungainly name if ever there was one.

1 large Spanish onion, chopped
6 fl oz/180 ml stock
Splash or two of medium sherry
1 large packet frozen diced swedes
2 tablespoons stock
4–6 fl oz/120–180 ml buttermilk

Purée from 1 head Baked Garlic
  (optional, see page 17)
Salt and pepper
½–1 teaspoon crumbled dried
  rosemary
Crushed chilli peppers to taste
  (optional)

1 Preheat oven to 350° F, 180° C, Gas Mark 4.
2 Combine onions, and 6 fl oz/180 ml stock in a heavy frying
   pan. Cover and bring to the boil. Boil rapidly for 5–7 minutes,
   until the onions are almost dry and beginning to brown.
   Uncover. Continue to cook, stirring, until the onions are
   sticking and browning. Pour in a splash of sherry, stir and
   scrape up the browned bits. When the onions are tender and
   amber brown, remove from the heat and set aside.
3 Defrost frozen swedes with 2 tablespoons stock in the microwave.
4 Place defrosted swedes with their liquid in a food processor.
   Add remaining ingredients, including sautéed onions. Process until very smooth.
5 Spread the mixture into a gratin dish, cover, and bake for 30
   minutes, until hot and bubbly.

❄ Ⓢ PURÉE OF SWEDE, TURNIP
AND
WHITE BEANS

Makes 3 pts/1800 ml purée

One of my favourite vegetarian meals consists of this purée,
Intense Mushroom Ragoût (page 118) and Creamy Spinach (*Slim
Cuisine I*).

3 carrots, chopped
1 large onion, chopped
2 stalks celery, chopped
3 cloves garlic, crushed
1 bay leaf
1 teaspoon herbes de Provence,
  crumbled
12 fl oz/360 ml stock
5 medium turnips, peeled and
  chopped

2 tins (14 oz/420 g each) white
  kidney beans (cannelini beans),
  drained
5 oz/150 g frozen diced swede,
  thawed, cooked according to
  packet directions
6 fl oz/180 ml fromage frais
Salt and freshly ground pepper to
  taste
⅕ pt/120 ml grated Parmesan
  cheese

1   Combine, carrots, onion, celery, garlic, bay leaf, herbes de Provence and 6 fl oz/180 ml stock in a large heavy-bottomed frying pan. Cover and bring to the boil. Reduce heat and simmer for 15–20 minutes until vegetables are tender. Uncover, raise heat, and cook until the liquid has evaporated and the vegetables are browning.
2   Stir in the turnips and the remaining stock. Cover and simmer until all vegetables are tender, about 15 minutes. Add beans.
3   Cook, uncovered, for 5 minutes more, until all the liquid is gone. Discard bay leaf. Season with salt and pepper.
4   Purée the vegetable mixture in the food processor. Process in the swede and the fromage frais. Correct seasonings.
5   Preheat oven to 400° F, 200° C, Gas Mark 6. Spread the vegetable purée in a gratin pan. Sprinkle with cheese. Bake uncovered for 30 minutes, until hot, bubbly and brown.

This freezes very well. Prepare the recipe as far as step 4, then cool and freeze. Bake from the frozen state at 400° F, 200° C, Gas Mark 6, covered for 30 minutes, uncovered for 30 minutes, or cook from the frozen state in the microwave (approximately 6 minutes on high), then flash under a hot grill to brown the top.

♡   Omit Parmesan cheese.

♡ ⊕   ## PAN-'FRIED' POTATOES
WITH ONIONS

Serves 2

1 large Spanish onion	*Salt and freshly ground pepper to*
Approximately 8 fl oz/240 ml stock	*taste*
8 small new potatoes, unpeeled	

1   Cut the onion into quarters. Slice each quarter crosswise into ½ inch/1.25 cm chunks.
2   Spread the onion chunks evenly over the bottom of a heavy non-reactive frying pan. Heat until sizzling and beginning to stick to the bottom of the pan.
3   While the onions are cooking, cut the new potatoes in half lengthwise, then slice crosswise into 4 inch/0.6 cm thick slices.
4   When the onions are sizzling and sticking, stir in 2 fl oz/60 ml of stock. Let it fume and foam and boil up, stirring up the browned bits in the frying pan as it does so. Boil, stirring, until just about dry.

5   Stir in most of the remaining stock. Stir in potatoes. Reduce heat to simmering.
6   Cover and allow to simmer gently for approximately 10 minutes.
7   Uncover and test a potato. If not yet tender, add a bit more stock, re-cover and simmer until tender but not falling apart.
8   Uncover, raise heat and cook, turning the potatoes occasionally, until they are browned. Season to taste and serve at once.

'Fire officers in Cambridgeshire want to banish chip pans from the county's kitchens. Grill it or bake it, but don't deep-fry it – that is the message from the Fire and Rescue Service.'

Cambridge Evening News

 ## 'FRIED' POTATOES

Serves 1 male teenager, or 3–4 normal people

I am constantly updating, revising and improving this perennial family favourite. Here is the up-to-the-minute version, quicker than the one in *Slim Cuisine I*. I hope one day to be able to remove a spud from the larder, eye it sternly and utter '"fry" yourself!', and it will immediately form itself into perfect grease-free chips. Until that unlikely time, this is the quickest and best I can do. I promise, these chips will amaze you. I can't make them often enough for my family.

---

2 large baking potatoes,   *Salt (optional)*
   approximately 12 oz/360 g each

---

1   Preheat oven to 400° F, 200° C, Gas Mark 6.
2   Scrub the potatoes but do not peel them. Pierce them in several places with a fork or thin skewer. Line the microwave carousel with a paper towel.
3   Place potatoes on the carousel. Microwave at full power for 6 minutes, turning the potatoes over after 3 minutes.
4   Remove the potatoes from the oven and allow to stand for 5 minutes.
5   With a sharp knife, cut each potato lengthwise into ¼–½ inch/0.6–1.25 cm thick strips. Arrange in one layer on one or two *non-stick* baking trays. Bake for approximately 20–30 minutes, turning the potatoes with tongs approximately halfway through, and shaking the tray every once in a while so that they do not stick. When they are beautifully browned and a bit puffy, they are done. Salt lightly if desired and serve.

'"He eats French fries," she says and sinks into the kitchen chair to Weep Her Heart Out once and for all. "He goes after school with Melvyn Weiner and stuffs himself with French-fried potatoes."'

Philip Roth, *Portnoy's Complaint*

♡ **ROAST POTATOES**

The better the stock, the better the roast potatoes. If you have any dripping left from a roast chicken (with the fat skimmed off, of course) try using it for roasting the potatoes instead of using plain stock.

Stock   *Salt and freshly ground pepper*
Small whole new potatoes, or
*   medium-sized potatoes, halved*
*   or quartered*

---

1   Preheat oven to 400° F, 200° C, Gas Mark 6.
2   Pour stock into a shallow baking dish to a depth of about ¼ inch/0.6 cm. Put the potatoes in the dish in one layer. Season with salt and pepper, and stir them around.
3   Bake uncovered for 40–50 minutes, shaking the pan and stirring occasionally. When they are browned and tender, they are done. (Pour a bit more stock into the dish as necessary during cooking.) Chopped garlic and onion may be added in step 1 if desired.

'"I haven't eaten potatoes for twenty-five years," said Frank in a far-off brooding tone . . .
   'The potatoes were brought. Not all the perfumes of Araby smelt so sweet. They ate them with their fingers.'

W. Somerset Maugham, *The Three Fat Women of Antibes*

♡ **KASHA WITH MUSHROOMS**

Makes 2 pts/1200 ml

Kasha is roasted buckwheat groats, available in many wholefood stores. I urge you to try kasha, and some of the other grains discussed in this collection. If you like rice, you'll *love* kasha, couscous, bulghur (cracked wheat) and polenta. They add important fibre and vitamin E (one of the fat soluble vitamins) to your diet, but – as important – they are delicious, easy to eat, a wonderful complement to all sorts of dishes, and each one of them is a serenity-producing food. My recipe for kasha is a classic one, except for the omission of egg yolks, and butter or chicken fat. It may be prepared without the dried mushrooms if desired; in that case use 16 fl oz/480 ml stock in step 6.

½ oz/15 g dried mushrooms (look for cèpes or the Italian counterpart, porcini)
½ lb/240 g fresh mushrooms, coarsely chopped
2 fl oz/60 ml stock
2 fl oz/60 ml dry sherry
Generous dash of soy sauce

1 Spanish onion, coarsely chopped
4 fl oz/120 ml stock
2 egg whites, lightly beaten
8 fl oz/240 ml kasha (roasted buckwheat groats)
8 fl oz/240 ml stock
Salt and freshly ground pepper to taste

1   Rinse the dried mushrooms well under cold running water. Soak in hot water to cover generously for at least an hour. Strain the water through a coffee filter, or a double cheese-cloth-lined sieve, and reserve. Briefly rinse the soaked mushrooms once more under cold water. Trim off and discard any tough stems. Coarsely chop the dried mushrooms.
2   Combine the soaked mushrooms, the fresh mushrooms, 2 fl oz/60 ml stock, the sherry and the soy sauce in a heavy non-reactive frying pan. Simmer briskly, stirring occasionally, until the liquid is almost gone, and the mushrooms are 'frying' in their own juices. Set aside.
3   Combine the onions and 4 fl oz/120 ml of stock in a heavy non-reactive frying pan. Cover and bring to the boil. Reduce heat a bit, and let simmer briskly for 5–7 minutes or until almost dry. Uncover and cook until beginning to stick and brown. Pour in a splash or two of stock and stir and scrape until the onions are beautifully brown, syrupy and tender. Add to the mushrooms.
4   Stir the egg white into the kasha. Mix until the grains are well coated with the egg.
5   Heat a large, heavy frying pan. With a wooden spoon or paddle stir the kasha in the pan, over moderate heat, until each grain is dry and separate. It will give off an appetizingly toasty aroma. This should take about 5 minutes. Scrape the kasha into a large pot that can be covered.
6   Combine the 8 fl oz/240 ml stock with 8 fl oz/240 ml reserved mushroom liquid, and bring to the boil.
7   Stir the boiling liquid into the kasha. Cover the pot and simmer over lowest heat for 30 minutes. Remove from the heat, uncover and drape a clean tea towel over the pot. Re-cover and

let stand for 5–10 minutes, until the liquid is absorbed and the kasha is fluffy and tender, with each grain separate.

8   Mix kasha, onions and mushrooms.

Note: This may be prepared in advance and reheated in the microwave or conventional oven. To make the classic and beloved Russian-Jewish dish kasha varnishkas, mix equal amounts of this kasha with freshly boiled and drained bowtie-shaped pasta.

♡   # WHEAT PILAF

Makes approximately 2 pts/1200 ml

Bulghur is available in wholefood shops, and most supermarkets as well. It is made from dried wheat berries that have been parched, steamed and crushed. Bulghur is chock full of fibre, and vitamin E, and has a gloriously nutty taste and texture. It complements many main dishes beautifully; try it with Chinese Beef (page 64) instead of the more obvious rice or try it with Chicken Liver Kebabs (page 86) or any stew.

1 Spanish onion, coarsely chopped	*8 fl oz/240 ml bulghur*
½ pt/300 ml stock	*½ pt/300 ml fresh strained orange*
½ teaspoon ground coriander	*juice*
½ teaspoon ground cumin	*Salt and freshly ground pepper to*
2 cloves garlic, minced	*taste*
Grated zest from ½ large orange	*Chopped fresh coriander (optional)*

1   Spread onion pieces in a heavy frying pan that can be covered. Heat gently. Cook at a moderate heat for a few minutes until the onions begin to sizzle and stick to the pan.

2   Stir in 4 fl oz/120 ml stock and let it bubble up as you stir and scrape up any browned bits. Stir in the spices and garlic. Simmer until the mixture is very thick and the onions are 'frying' in their own juices. Zest the ½ orange right over the onions so that the zest goes in with some oils. Add the bulghur and stir until everything is well combined. Bring the remaining stock to a boil with the orange juice and add it to the wheat. Season with salt and pepper.

3   Cover the pan and simmer over lowest heat for about 20 minutes, until the bulghur is tender but not mushy, and all the liquid is absorbed. Fluff with a fork. To serve, mound on a warm plate or spoon into a warm bowl. Garnish with coriander.

MANGO AND TOMATO
SALAD

Serves 4

If the mango is ripe, and the tomatoes are *real* tomatoes, not those pathetic impostors often found in supermarkets, this salad will scintillate. Serve it as a separate course.

---

6 small tomatoes	*Dressing (see below)*
1 mango	

---

1   With a sharp knife slice straight down on the mango, slicing it through, but missing the large flat centre stone to which quite a bit of mango flesh clings. Repeat on the other side of the stone.
2   Carefully peel the skin from both halves. Slice each half thinly to produce long strips of mango and set aside.
3   Peel the skin from the mango flesh around the stone and put the flesh in a small bowl along with any juices and set aside to use in the dressing.
4   Arrange the tomato slices in two rows around the perimeter of a pretty dish. Fill the centre with overlapping mango slices. Pass the dressing separately.

Dressing

---

2 tablespoons fromage frais	*Pinch of dry mustard*
2 tablespoons wine vinegar	*Excess mango flesh and juice (see*
1 tablespoon buttermilk	*above)*
Dash of Worcestershire sauce	*Pinch or two of brown sugar, to taste*

Whisk together all ingredients except the excess mango and the sugar. Put them in the container of the liquidizer together with the mango flesh and juice. Blend until perfectly smooth. Taste and blend in a pinch or two of brown sugar if necessary. Refrigerate until needed.

 # SPICY POTATO SALAD

Serves 6

Cold potatoes don't have to nestle under a mantle of that evil ointment – mayonnaise. Egg yolks and oil . . . I ask you! You might as well trowel it on your hips and have done with it. Try this creamy, herby, spicy dressing instead.

135

1½ lb/720 g boiling potatoes,
    unpeeled, steamed until tender
    but not mushy
2 tablespoons fresh lime juice
1 teaspoon soy sauce
¼ teaspoon cayenne pepper
½ teaspoon cumin
1 teaspoon caraway seeds
2 stalks celery, diced
1 carrot, coarsely grated

½ small red pepper, peeled and
    diced
½ small red pepper, peeled and
    diced
½ small yellow pepper, peeled and
    diced
Salt and freshly ground pepper to
    taste
Dressing (see below)

1   Cool the potatoes to lukewarm. Cut into 1 inch/2.5 cm cubes.
    Toss with the lime juice, soy sauce and spices.
2   Gently combine potatoes with the remaining ingredients.
    Chill.

'Shall we go to Schrafft's . . . where they have mayonnaise in
fiascos?'

E. B. White, *Across the Street and Into the Grill*

Dressing

3 tablespoons yoghurt
1 tablespoon buttermilk
3 spring onions, trimmed and sliced
    thin

1 tablespoon snipped chives
1 tablespoon chopped parsley

Combine thoroughly.

♡ MARINATED PEPPERS

Makes 2 pts/1200 ml

One of the best marinated vegetable dishes I know, and perfect for
an elegant picnic.

6 large peppers (a combination of
    red, yellow and orange) cut into
    ¾ inch/2 cm strips and peeled

2 fl oz/60 ml balsamic vinegar
1 tablespoon caster sugar
Salt to taste (be very sparing)

1   Place the pepper strips in a shallow dish.
2   Combine the vinegar and sugar and stir to dissolve the sugar.

Pour the mixture over the peppers and toss well. Sprinkle with a modest amount of salt.

3   Refrigerate for at least 12 hours. Shake the dish or stir the peppers, when you think of it. Serve cold.

♡ 🐻 🕐 MARINATED CARROTS

Makes 1 pt/600 ml

Devotees of Slim Cuisine soon become carrot fiends; the beautiful orange root is so crisp, sweet and good tasting, and you can eat all you want. In some cultures, some form of sliced carrots are always eaten for luck at the New Year, because the slices resemble golden coins.

1 lb/480 g carrots, peeled and sliced ¼ inch/0.6 cm thick	Pinch or two of ground cayenne (or to taste)
3 cloves garlic, very coarsely chopped	Pinch or two of cinnamon
⅕ pt/120 ml wine vinegar	Pinch or two of allspice
¼ teaspoon ground cumin	Salt and freshly ground pepper to taste
	2 tablespoons chopped parsley

1   Steam the carrots and garlic over boiling water for 5–10 minutes until the carrots are crisp-tender. Cool under cold running water and drain well.
2   While the carrots are steaming, combine the vinegar with the ground spices. Shake well.
3   Toss together the carrots, vinegar mixture and parsley. Refrigerate until needed. Serve cold or at room temperature.

♡ 🕐 CREAMY HERB DRESSING

Makes 12 fl oz/360 ml

A lovely salad cream for all sorts of salads. To use as a mayonnaise-type sandwich spread, omit the buttermilk.

4 fl oz/120 ml quark	1 teaspoon Dijon mustard or New York Deli Mustard (page 138)
4 fl oz/120 ml fromage frais	1 tablespoon freshly chopped parsley
4 fl oz/120 ml buttermilk	Freshly ground pepper to taste
Dash Worcestershire sauce	

Whisk all ingredients together. Refrigerate.

NEW YORK DELI MUSTARD

Makes 8 fl oz/240 ml

Home-made mustard is habit-forming. Once you've tried it, you will want to have a jar in the fridge always. It's good as a sandwich spread, a dip, or a sauce.

5 level tablespoons dry mustard	*2 tablespoons dark brown sugar*
2 fl oz/60 ml mustard seeds	*1 teaspoon salt*
4 fl oz/120 ml warm water	*¼ teaspoon ground ginger*
8 fl oz/240 ml cider vinegar	*¼ teaspoon ground allspice*
1 large garlic clove, peeled and	*¼ teaspoon ground cinnamon*
* crushed*	

1 Whisk together the dry mustard, mustard seeds and 4 fl oz/120 ml warm water in a heavy non-reactive saucepan. Set aside.
2 In a second non-reactive saucepan, combine all the remaining ingredients. Bring to a boil, reduce the heat and simmer gently for 5 minutes. Let cool for 2 or 3 minutes. Whisk the spiced vinegar into the mustard.
3 Bring to a simmer and simmer very gently, stirring frequently, for 10 minutes; it should just bubble gently around the edges. With a rubber spatula, scrape the mixture into a bowl. Let stand for 2 hours.
4 Scrape the mustard into the container of a food processor. Process to a grainy purée.
5 Scrape the mustard into a jar. Cover and allow to mellow overnight at room temperature. Store in the refrigerator.

'There was often no money at all and we existed on dry bread rubbed with garlic . . . As a change we had bread smeared with mustard, when there was any mustard.'

Theodora FitzGibbon, *With Love*

138

Sweet Things and Drinks

'Mrs Mayfair gorged herself on three desserts and kept saying "Just a sliver, that's all. Just a sliver!" when the chocolate cake went round.

'"Poor Henrietta", Mrs Prescott said, watching her enormous sister-in-law spooning down ice cream. "It's that psychosomatic hunger they're always talking about. Makes her eat so."'

Sylvia Plath, *The Day Mr Prescott Died*

PLUM JAM

Approximately ½ pt/300 ml

This is an easy and fresh-tasting almost instant plum jam, that will brighten the breakfast table, or make a simple pudding stirred into fromage frais. With good bread, and jam like this, why would you want to grease things up with butter or margarine?

16 fl oz/480 ml chunked, unpeeled plums (golden, red, or purple)	*Approximately 1 tablespoon sugar Lemon juice (optional)*

1   Mash the plums with a potato masher, until they are a lumpy purée. Spread the purée in a shallow dish and sprinkle with sugar. Let sit for 30 minutes.
2   Stir and taste. Add a squirt of lemon juice, if the taste needs sharpening. Serve spread on toast.

PRUNES IN LEMON SAUCE

Makes 10 fl oz/300 ml

Mention prunes in the United States, and everyone snickers and looks vaguely embarrassed. Somehow prunes have become associated with geriatric diets and 'regularity', and no one wants to admit their lusciousness and versatility. Go figure it out!

½ lb/240 g large prunes 1 piece (2 inches/5 cm long) cinnamon stick	*1 pt/600 ml strong lemon verbena tea ½–1 tablespoon sugar 1 small lemon*

1   Put the prunes and cinnamon stick in a saucepan. Pour in tea and bring to the boil. Reduce heat and simmer, covered, for 15 minutes.
2   Uncover and stir in sugar, and the juice of ½ lemon. Slice the other ½ lemon and add the slices. Simmer, uncovered, for 10–15 minutes more. If a lot of juices remain, drain the prunes and boil the juices for 5 minutes. Re-combine. Serve warm or cold, with yoghurt or fromage frais if desired.

STRAWBERRIES IN RASPBERRY SAUCE

♡ ⊕

Serve each diner a heap of fresh strawberries, a puddle of Raspberry Sauce (see below) and a cloud of low-fat fromage frais. The drill is to pick up a berry by its green stem, dip it in the puddle, dabble it in the cloud, and pop it in the mouth. If you and someone you love share this berry feast, pop them into each other's mouths. Sheer heaven!

Raspberry Sauce

Makes 16 fl oz/480 ml

---

2 boxes (12 oz/360 g each) frozen raspberries, thawed and drained   *Nutra Sweet (Canderel) to taste*

---

1   Purée the berries in the liquidizer.
2   Pour into a sieve and rub through. Discard the seeds.
3   Stir in sweetener (2–3 tablespoons) to taste. Refrigerate until needed.

Variation: Strawberry Fondue

Serve each diner a bowl of whole strawberries with the stems still on, a bowl of fromage frais, a bowl of Chocolate Cream Sauce (page 154), and a bowl of Raspberry Sauce (above), then allow your guests to dip and nibble at will.

'To get back to the sublime, one will always dine on lucullan dishes, but as if Lucullus had rounded up a new type of health food; melons from the Pace gardens, wild strawberries gathered from the slopes of the Dardanelles; raspberries as big as crabapples . . .'

Anita Loos, *The Italians Have a Word for It*

CHERRIES IN HONEYED CREAM

Serves 4

Fruit in the freezer and fromage frais in the fridge should be facts of your kitchen life. Never be without them. What is life, after all, without pudding? Look for the frozen cherries in frozen food shops such as Bejam.

1 package frozen dark cherries	*6 fl oz/180 ml fromage frais*
1½ tablespoons honey	*1 teaspoon brown sugar*
½ teaspoon vanilla essence	

1   Thaw the berries until their juices begin to flow, but they are still icy cold. Arrange an equal amount of berries and their juices in each of 4 glass bowls.
2   While the berries are thawing, gently fold the honey and vanilla into the fromage frais.
3   Pour the fromage frais evenly over each serving of berries. Sprinkle each evenly with ¼ teaspoon of brown sugar. Let it stand for 5 minutes before serving.

⊠ ⏲ Thaw cherries in the microwave.

♡ Omit honey – substitute low-Calorie sweetener if desired.

POACHED PEARS IN HONEYED RED WINE

Serves 6

Pears poached in wine take on a beautiful red-purple glow. I love the way they look standing on white plates in a pool of their sauce.

1 pt/600 ml red wine	*Juice from 1 lemon*
1 teaspoon vanilla essence	*¼ teaspoon cinnamon*
3 tablespoons honey	*6 ripe but firm pears*
Grated zest from ½ lemon	

1   Preheat oven to 375° F, 190° C, Gas Mark 5.
2   Combine wine, vanilla, honey, all the lemon zest, half the lemon juice, and cinnamon, in a non-reactive pot. Bring to the boil, stirring occasionally. Reduce heat, partially cover, and simmer for 15 minutes.
3   Have ready a bowl of water to which you have added the remaining lemon juice. Peel the pears, but leave them whole. As they are peeled, drop them in the bowl of water. When all are peeled, put them in a baking dish. Pour the wine mixture over them. Cover and bake for 30–45 minutes, until tender but not mushy. Baste the pears occasionally. Cool, then refrigerate. They will keep for days. Serve cold.

Airy Pleasures

Soufflés are dramatic, gossamer creations, although the thought of making one fills many novice cooks with fear and trembling. A soufflé's spectacular appearance – and the blissful sighs that greet it as it emerges from the kitchen in all its airy glory – make soufflé cookery very gratifying indeed. Ignore all the stories you have heard about their unpredictability and their penchant for collapsing from the vibrations of a footstep. Soufflés are really very easy to produce.

I must also tell you to ignore most of the usual rules of soufflé cookery. Traditionally, they are made with an egg yolk enriched base. Egg yolks contain fat and the base is usually a thick white sauce – rich in butter and cream. To bring the fat level even higher, the soufflé dish is always liberally buttered or oiled.

I had a glorious time breaking all the rules, and I've come up with some beauties. They rise to spectacular heights, they taste *intensely* of their main ingredient, and – although they collapse if left to stand, as do all soufflés – they do not collapse as pathetically as do traditional ones. Should there be any leftover soufflé (you may have to hide it in an opaque plastic container and label it 'tripes in prune sauce'), it is delicious served (cut into wedges) on the next day, with no apologies needed. It will be a lovely, spongy pudding.

Here are a few helpful soufflé hints:

1   Beaten egg whites folded into a fruit base (or combined with cocoa, page 155) cause the soufflé's magical rise in the oven. The eggs should be beaten with a wire whip (an electric mixer with a wire whip attachment is the ideal) in an immaculately clean bowl. The slightest trace of grease (luckily, there will be no grease in *your* kitchen) or egg yolk will prevent the egg whites from expanding. Have the egg whites at room temperature; cold egg whites will not whip up to maximum volume.

2   Always be sure that there is no oven shelf above the soufflé. These beauties really rise, and you may open the oven to find your soufflé has left its dish and is hanging from the upper shelf. Give it plenty of head room.

3   A baking soufflé is not as temperamental as you might imagine. You may walk around the kitchen, and even talk out loud while it is baking. I wouldn't dance the fandango in front of the oven, however.

4   Bake it until it has risen impressively and a thin skewer inserted near the centre comes out *almost* clean. Or – if you prefer a very firm soufflé – when the skewer emerges clean.

5   Have everyone seated and ready. Serve *at once*.

'The words people use for a Chartres or a Mozart,
He's using to praise a soufflé.'

Judith Viorst, *The Gourmet*

BANANA SOUFFLÉ
Serves 4–6

---

3 medium-sized ripe bananas
1 tablespoon dark rum
½ teaspoon nutmeg
½ teaspoon cinnamon
1 scant tablespoon lemon juice
8 egg whites, at room temperature

Pinch of cream of tartar
Approximately 2 tablespoons sugar
 (less if the bananas are very
 sweet)
½ teaspoon vanilla

---

1   Preheat oven to 350° F, 180° C, Gas Mark 4.
2   Cut bananas into thick slices. Purée with the rum, the spices
     and the lemon juice in a food processor or blender. Scrape into
     a large bowl.
3   Beat egg whites in an electric mixer on medium speed until
     foamy. Add cream of tartar and beat on highest speed, adding
     sugar a little at a time, until the sugar is dissolved and the
     whites are shiny and thick and hold firm peaks. Fold in the
     vanilla.
4   Gently fold the whites into the banana mixture.
5   Spoon the banana mixture into 5½–6 pt/3300–3600 ml soufflé
     dish. Cook on the middle shelf of the oven for 30–35 minutes.
     (Remove the top shelf first.) Serve at once.

Note: If you wish to gild the lily, serve with Chocolate Cream
Sauce (page 154), or Raspberry Sauce (page 141).

Ⓢ   # MANGO SOUFFLÉ
Serves 4–6

---

3 large ripe mangoes, peeled, pitted
   and chopped
1½ teaspoons lime juice
2 tablespoons cornflour

2 fl oz/60 ml water
3 tablespoons dark rum
2 tablespoons sugar
8 egg whites, at room temperature

---

1   Purée mangoes and lime juice in the food processor.
2   Combine cornflour and water and whisk until a smooth paste.
3   Stir into the mango mixture. Bring to the boil. Reduce heat and
     simmer for 4–5 minutes, until very thick.

4	Stir in rum and 1 tablespoon sugar and cook for 1 minute more. Scrape into a large bowl and leave to cool.
5	Beat egg whites in an electric mixer on medium speed until foamy. Add remaining sugar, a little at a time, while beating on highest speed, until the sugar is dissolved and the whites are shiny and thick and hold firm peaks.
6	Gently fold the whites into the mango mixture.
7	Spoon the mango mixture into a 5½–6 pt (3300–3600 ml) soufflé dish. Cook on the middle shelf of the oven for 35–40 minutes. (Remove the top shelf first.) Serve at once.

CHOCOLATE SOUFFLÉ

Serves 6

I would not be worthy of my mission in life if I were not able to come up with a decadent-tasting chocolate dessert like this every once in a while. Ignore rumours you may have heard about carob being a good substitute for chocolate. As far as I'm concerned, carob is an abomination on the face of the earth. This is the *real thing*. Eat it and weep.

9 tablespoons caster sugar	9 egg whites, at room temperature
9 tablespoons unsweetened,	Pinch of cream of tartar
fat-reduced cocoa (see page 155)	1½ teaspoons of vanilla
	1½ teaspoons dark rum

1	Preheat the oven to 350° F, 180° C, Gas Mark 4.
2	Sift together all of the sugar except about 2 tablespoons with all of the cocoa. Set aside.
3	In an electric mixer, beat the egg whites with the cream of tartar until foamy. At highest speed, continue beating, adding the 2 tablespoons of plain sugar a little at a time, until the whites hold stiff peaks.
4	With a rubber spatula, fold the sugar-cocoa mixture into the beaten whites. Fold in the vanilla and rum.
5	Pile the egg white mixture into a 5½–6 pt/3300–3600 ml soufflé dish. Bake in the centre of the oven (remove the top shelf) for 30–40 minutes. *Serve at once.* (Pass a jug of Raspberry Sauce, page 141, if desired.)

Variation: Fudgy Chocolate Torte
To make a chocolate cake follow the recipe above but use a 10 inch/25 cm non-stick flan tin instead of a soufflé dish and bake for 20–30 minutes. (A skewer inserted near the middle should emerge

not quite clean.) Remove from the oven and let the tin cool on a rack. Serve wedges of this dense torte on pools of Raspberry Sauce (page 141), topped with Chocolate Cream Sauce (page 154), and garnished with a few raspberries.

'. . . the Chocolate Elite – the select millions who like chocolate in all its infinite variety, using "like" as in "I like to breathe."'

Sandra Boynton, *Chocolate the Consuming Passion*

CHOCOLATE MERINGUES

Makes 100

These delightfully crunchy little morsels work out at about 10 Calories each. The chocolate taste is very intense.

3 egg whites, at room temperature	*1 teaspoon vanilla essence*
Pinch of cream of tartar and salt	*4 tablespoons fat-reduced cocoa,*
5 oz/150 g sugar	*(see page 155) sifted*

1   Preheat oven to 225° F, 120° C, Gas Mark 1.
2   Beat egg whites with cream of tartar and salt until foamy. Increase speed. Beat, adding sugar, 1–2 tablespoons at a time, until shiny and stiff and firm peaks hold. Fold in vanilla and cocoa.
3   Line two baking sheets with greaseproof paper. Drop batter on sheets by the half teaspoonful, 1 inch/2.5 cm apart. Bake for 45 minutes. (To make small nests, make a dent in each dollop of batter with a spoon before baking.)
4   Turn oven off. Leave in the oven for at least 3 hours. (They may stay in overnight.) Do not open the door until the time is up.

Variation I: White Meringues
Follow the above recipe but omit the cocoa. The meringue mixture – chocolate or white – can be made into free form shapes, or piped through a pastry bag in order to make bunnies, etc.

Variation II: Meringue Pie Shell
Use a rubber spatula to scrape the meringue mixture into an ungreased 9 inch/23 cm pie pan (do not use one with a detachable bottom), and smooth it over the bottom and up the sides. Bake for 1 hour and cool as above. The shell will have a wonderfully fudgy texture.

146

FRENCH TOAST

Serves 6

In the United States, French toast is eaten as a festive breakfast (almost all breakfasts are festive in the US) with lashings of pure maple syrup. It also makes a lovely pudding, or a teatime treat. I have edited out the cream and butter of the traditional version, but the texture is still voluptuously custardy.

6 oz/180 g 1–2 day old bakery white bread	*Pinch of nutmeg (optional)*
3 eggs	*Pinch of salt*
2 egg whites	*Caster sugar or icing sugar (optional)*
16 fl oz/480 skimmed milk	

1   Slice bread. Cut each slice in half. Neatly arrange slices, overlapping, in an 8 inch/20 cm square, 1–2 inch/2–5 cm deep baking dish.
2   Beat the eggs and whites. Gently beat in milk, nutmeg and salt. Pour the mixture over the bread. Use a broad spatula to push the bread into the liquid. Be careful not to break up the bread. Cover the dish and refrigerate overnight.
3   Remove the dish from the refrigerator and let it stand while you preheat the oven to 350° F, 180° C, Gas Mark 4. Put the kettle on to boil.
4   Choose a baking dish larger than the one with the bread. Put it in the preheated oven. Put the bread dish in the larger dish. Pour boiling water in the larger dish to come about halfway up the sides of the smaller dish. Bake for 30–40 minutes, until puffed and firm. (A knife inserted near the centre will emerge clean.)
5   Serve at once with a sprinkling of caster sugar or a small sifting of icing sugar on each serving, if desired.

BREAD PUDDING

Serves 6

Talk about voluptuous custard! This is VC to the max. Bread pudding is nursery food's finest expression. *Everyone* loves this, indeed, some may weep a nostalgic tear or two on to their plates.

6 oz/180 g 1–2 day old unsliced bakery white bread	16 fl oz/480 ml skimmed milk
3 eggs	1 teaspoon vanilla essence
2 egg whites	Pinch or two of cinnamon
3½–4 tablespoons caster sugar	(optional)

1   Cut bread into ¾–1 inch/2–2.5 cm chunks. Put them in an 8 inch/20 cm square, 1–2 inch/2.5–5 cm deep baking dish.

2   Beat the eggs and whites with the sugar. Gently beat in the milk and flavourings. Pour the mixture over the bread. Use a broad spatula to push the bread into the liquid. Stir it all up, but be careful not to break up the bread. Cover the dish and refrigerate for several hours (or overnight).

3   Remove the dish from the refrigerator, and let stand at room temperature while you preheat the oven to 350° F, 180° C, Gas Mark 4. Put the kettle on to boil.

4   Choose a baking dish larger than the one with the bread. Put it in the preheated oven. Put the bread dish in the larger dish. Pour boiling water in the larger dish to come about halfway up the sides of the smaller dish. Bake for 30–40 minutes, until puffed and firm. (A knife inserted near the centre will emerge clean.)

5   Cool the bread pudding on a rack. Serve warm or at room temperature.

CHOCOLATE BREAD PUDDING

Serves 6

Bread pudding, cocoa and dried fruit *put together!* Who could ask for anything more?

6 oz/180 g unsliced bakery wholemeal bread	4½–5 tablespoons dark brown sugar
3 tablespoons sultanas	1 tablespoon sifted unsweetened fat-reduced cocoa (see page 155)
7 dried figs or pitted prunes, chopped coarsely	¼ teaspoon ground cinnamon
	1 teaspoon vanilla essence
5 egg whites	16 fl oz/480 ml skimmed milk

1   Cut the bread into ¾–1 inch/2–2.5 cm chunks. Spread them out in an 8 inch/20 cm square, 1½–2 inch (4–5 cm) deep baking dish with the sultanas and prunes.

2   Beat the egg whites with the sugar. Sprinkle in the cocoa and flavourings. Beat to blend. Gently beat in the milk. Pour the mixture over the bread. Use a broad spatula to push the bread

into the liquid. Stir it all up, but be careful not to break up the bread. Cover the dish and refrigerate for several hours (or overnight).

3   Remove the dish from the refrigerator, and let stand at room temperature while you preheat the oven to 350° F, 180° C, Gas Mark 4. Put the kettle on to boil.

4   Choose a baking dish larger than the one with the bread. Put it in the preheated oven. Put the bread dish in the larger dish. Pour boiling water in the larger dish to come about halfway up the sides of the smaller dish. Bake for 30–40 minutes, until puffed and firm.

5   Cool the bread pudding on a rack. Serve warm or at room temperature.

BREAD PUDDING WITH MINCEMEAT

Serves 6

I developed this for the BBC's 'Daytime Live' as a Slim Cuisine substitute for Easter's hot cross buns.

6 oz/180 g 1–2 day old unsliced bakery white bread	*1 teaspoon vanilla essence*
4 eggs	*Pinch or two of cinnamon or mixed spice*
3½–4 tablespoons caster sugar	*6 oz/180 g Slim Cuisine Mincemeat (see following recipe)*
16 fl oz/480 g skimmed milk	

1   Cut bread into ¾–1 inch/2–2.5 cm chunks. Put them in an 8 inch/20 cm square, 1–2 inch/2.5–5 cm deep baking dish.

2   Beat the eggs with the sugar. Beat in the milk and flavourings. Stir in the fruit mix. Pour the mixture over the bread. Use a broad spatula to push the bread into the liquid. Stir it all up, but be careful not to break up the bread. Cover the dish and refrigerate for several hours (or overnight).

3   Remove the dish from the refrigerator, and let stand at room temperature while you preheat the oven to 350° F, 180° C, Gas Mark 4. Put the kettle on to boil.

4   Choose a baking dish larger than the one with the bread. Put it in the preheated oven. Put the bread dish in the larger dish. Pour boiling water in the larger dish to come about halfway up the sides of the smaller dish. Bake for 30–40 minutes, until puffed and firm. (A knife inserted near the centre will emerge clean.)

5   Cool the bread pudding on a rack. Serve warm or at room temperature.

⊞ ⊕ SLIM CUISINE MINCEMEAT

Makes 2½ pts/1500 ml

---

1 packet (18 oz/500 g) cake fruit
    (finely minced mixed dried
    fruit); the mix you choose should
    include sultanas, currants,
    orange and lemon peel
1 packet (9 oz/250 g) dried apricots,
    coarsely chopped (use scissors)

1 packet (5 oz/125 g) dried apple
    chunks, coarsely chopped (use
    scissors)
½ teaspoon each ground cinnamon,
    allspice and nutmeg
2 fl oz/60 ml each medium sherry
    and brandy
4 fl oz/120 ml water

---

1   Combine all ingredients and mix well.
2   Pour into a 4 pt/2400 ml soufflé dish. Cover with cling film.
    Pierce the cling film and microwave on high for 4 minutes,
    stirring once halfway through.

Note: This mixture will keep, well covered in the refrigerator, for
months. It improves with age.

Mince pies. Use this mixture inside filo pastry triangles. See page
39 for instructions for using filo.

FRUIT COMPÔTE

Makes 1 pt/600 ml

As good for breakfast as for dessert.

---

4 tablespoons sultanas
1 lb/480 g mixed dried fruit (dried
    apricots, apples, figs, prunes,
    pears)
8 fl oz/240 ml dry white wine
1½ oz/45 g caster sugar

½ cinnamon stick
Juice and grated zest of 1 lemon
Fromage frais, yoghurt, or Lemon
    Cream Sauce (see following
    recipe)

---

1   Combine the raisins, fruit, 8 fl oz/240 ml water, and the wine,
    in a baking dish. Allow to soak for 1 hour.
2   Preheat the oven to 350° F, 180° C, Gas Mark 4.
3   At the end of the hour, stir in the sugar, cinnamon stick, and
    lemon juice and zest. Cover the dish and bake for 1 hour. Serve
    warm or cold with fromage frais, yoghurt, or Lemon Cream
    Sauce.

LEMON CREAM SAUCE

Approximately ½ pt/300 ml sauce

The perfect topping for a dried fruit compôte, or for fresh fruit salads.

---

4 fl oz/120 ml water	*2 tablespoons buttermilk*
Grated zest of ½ lemon	*⅖ pt/240 ml drained fromage frais*
4 tablespoons fresh lemon juice	*½–1 tablespoon honey*

---

1   Combine water, lemon zest and lemon juice in a small saucepan. Boil, uncovered, until reduced to about 4 tablespoons. Cool.
2   Beat the lemon infusion and buttermilk into the fromage frais. Beat in the honey. Store in the refrigerator until needed.

BRÛLÉE OF CARAMELIZED BANANAS

Serves 12

The more I experiment with very low-fat cookery, the more amazed and delighted I am. Both these banana puddings are so over-the-top delicious, they taste almost decadent. Both may be served hot or cold, but the soufflé is definitely at its best (and most dramatic) when hot and inflated. And both puddings may be served with Raspberry Sauce (page 141) or Blackcurrant Sauce (*Slim Cuisine I*).

Banana base ingredients	*Few drops lemon juice*
6 large bananas, ripe but firm	*½ teaspoon vanilla essence*
Juice of ½ lime	*½ teaspoon orange liqueur or dark*
Juice of ½ large lemon	*rum*
3 fl oz/90 ml fresh orange juice	*4 egg whites, at room temperature*
1½ tablespoons orange liqueur or	*Pinch of cream of tartar*
dark rum	*¾ pt/480 ml fromage frais, in a*
1 rounded tablespoon dark brown	*large bowl*
sugar	*½ tablespoon dry wholemeal*
	breadcrumbs
Topping ingredients	*½ tablespoon brown sugar*
1½ very ripe bananas, peeled and	
sliced	

---

1   Prepare base: Preheat the grill to its highest setting.
2   Peel the bananas and cut in half lengthwise, then cut each half in half crosswise.

3 Put the juices and liqueur in a shallow baking dish or gratin dish that can hold the bananas in one layer. Turn the bananas in the juice, then arrange them in one layer, cut side down. Sprinkle evenly with the sugar.

4 Grill, 3 inches/8 cm from the heat, for 5 minutes, or until the bananas are well browned on top. Drain liquid into a small frying pan. Arrange the bananas, cut side down, in an attractive gratin dish. Boil the drained juices rapidly until very thick and syrupy. Be careful not to scorch them. Pour and scrape over the bananas. Set aside.

5 Prepare brûlée topping: purée the grilled bananas in the liquidizer with the lemon juice, vanilla and the liqueur. The mixture should be very smooth.

6 In a spotlessly clean bowl, with an electric mixer, beat the egg whites until they are foamy. Add a pinch of cream of tartar and beat until they hold soft peaks.

7 Continue beating, adding the puréed banana a bit at a time. Stop and scrape down the sides of the bowl occasionally. When all the puréed banana has been added and the egg whites are creamy, greatly expanded, and hold firm peaks, scrape them into the bowl of fromage frais.

8 With a large rubber spatula, fold the egg whites and fromage frais together, turning the bowl as you fold. Spread this mixture over the grilled bananas in the gratin dish, swirling it into decorative peaks. Sprinkle evenly with the breadcrumbs and sugar.

9 Grill, 3 inches/8 cm from the heat, for 3–4 minutes, until browned. Serve at once, or chill and serve later.

Variation: Soufflé of Caramelized Bananas

Prepare the grilled banana base as outlined in the previous recipe.

Topping ingredients	4 egg whites, at room temperature
3 large very ripe bananas	Pinch of cream of tartar
Juice of ½ lemon	2 tablespoons fromage frais
½ teaspoon each vanilla essence and orange liqueur or dark rum	½ tablespoon each brown sugar, dry wholemeal breadcrumbs

1 Preheat the oven to 350° F, 180° C, Gas Mark 4.

2 Purée the bananas with the lemon juice, vanilla and orange liqueur or rum in the liquidizer.

3 In an impeccably clean bowl, with an impeccably clean electric beater, beat the egg whites until foamy. Add cream of tartar and beat until the egg whites hold soft peaks.

4 Add puréed bananas a little at a time as you beat. Stop

occasionally to scrape down the sides. When all the puréed bananas have been added and the egg whites have greatly expanded, are creamy and hold firm peaks, stop beating.

5   Spoon the fromage frais over the beaten whites. With a rubber spatula, gently scrape the fromage frais over the surface of the whites in a thin layer. With the spatula, gently fold the layer of fromage frais into the whites.

6   Spread the mixture evenly over the grilled bananas. Sprinkle evenly with sugar and breadcrumbs. Bake (give it plenty of head room) for approximately 15 minutes, until dramatically puffed, and the juices are starting to bubble up through the soufflé topping. Serve *at once*, to gasps of delight.

'But there is something missing in any cuisine that asks us to think of a banana as a portion of potassium. There is something skewed about an eating regimen designed to do the most for every part of your body except the tip of your tongue.'

Ellen Goodman, *Washington Post*

SEMOLINA PUDDING – COLD VERSION

Makes 1⅕ pts/720 ml

Semolina pudding is one of those nursery dishes that induce tranquillity. It is hard to decide which is better, the cold version or the warm one. It is probably the one you are eating at the time.

⅖ pt/240 ml couscous	1 tablespoon plain gelatine
16 fl oz/480 ml skimmed milk	⅕ pt/120 ml warm water
3 oz/90 g caster sugar	14 fl oz/420 ml fromage frais
1 cinnamon stick	

1   Combine couscous, milk, sugar and cinnamon stick in a heavy-bottomed saucepan. Whisk together well. Slowly bring to the boil, stirring very frequently. Do not let it scorch.

2   Turn heat to its lowest point and simmer for about 5 minutes, stirring frequently, until thick and cooked. Remove from heat and let it rest for 5 minutes.

3   While the couscous is resting, dissolve the gelatine in the warm water.

4   Stir the gelatine thoroughly into the semolina. Discard the cinnamon stick. Cool the mixture to room temperature.

5   Thoroughly fold in the fromage frais. Pour into a glass bowl. Chill for several hours or overnight.

SEMOLINA PUDDING –
WARM VERSION

Makes 1pt 4fl oz/720 ml

When you need gentleness, love, warm understanding and something soft and sweet to cry into, this is your pudding. Or make it for a good friend who is going through a difficult patch.

---

8 fl oz/240 ml couscous	*1 cinnamon stick*
16 fl oz/480 ml skimmed milk	*14 fl oz/420 ml fromage frais, at*
3 oz/90 g caster sugar	*room temperature*

---

1   Combine couscous, milk, sugar and cinnamon stick in a heavy-bottomed saucepan. Whisk together well. Slowly bring to the boil, stirring very frequently. Do not let it scorch.
2   Turn heat to its lowest point and simmer for about 5 minutes, stirring frequently, until thick and cooked. Remove from heat and let it rest for 15 minutes.
3   Fold in the fromage frais. Serve at once.

Variations
1   Both the warm and cold version may be served with Chocolate Cream Sauce (see below) or Raspberry Sauce (page 141).
2   Serve the warm version with a spoonful of jam (see Plum Jam, page 140) stirred in. This version makes a super breakfast, when you want to start the day in a relaxed way. But if you have to be tough and hard for the work jungle, choose another breakfast. This one will turn you into an adorable and sweet pussycat for hours.

CHOCOLATE CREAM
SAUCE

Makes 1¼ pts/750 ml

Don't ever feel sorry for yourself because you are living on a low-fat diet. Make this sauce occasionally. Should self-pity threaten to overcome you, rush to the kitchen and whip up a batch of Banana Ice Cream (page 158). Pour some of this sauce into a large goblet. Scoop in some Banana Ice Cream. Pour a bit of Raspberry Sauce on top (page 141), and crumble on a Chocolate Meringue (page 146). Eat with a large spoon while grinning foolishly.

16 fl oz/480 ml skimmed milk	3–4 tablespoons unsweetened
4 tablespoons caster sugar	fat-reduced cocoa powder, sieved
2 tablespoons cornflour	(see below)
1 teaspoon vanilla essence	½ large orange
1½ tablespoons orange liqueur	4 fl oz/120 ml fromage frais
(Grand Marnier or Cointreau)	

1   Pour 12 fl oz/360 ml milk into a heavy non-stick pan. Heat very gently. Add sugar and stir over low heat until dissolved.
2   Stir together the cornflour with 4 fl oz/120 ml cold milk. Stir into hot milk-sugar mixture. Stir and cook over low heat until thick. Continue cooking and stirring for 1–2 minutes more. Stir in vanilla and orange liqueur. Scrape into a large bowl.
3   Off the heat, stir in the cocoa powder gradually. When it is well incorporated, zest the orange right over the bowl so that the zest and some of the orange oil go into the mixture. Let cool until barely warm.
4   Fold the fromage frais into the chocolate mixture. Scrape into a bowl. Chill with a piece of cling film directly on the surface to prevent a skin forming.

'No sooner had he wiped the whipped cream from his lips before a plate mountain-high in ice cream, bristling with macaroons, was thrust before him.'

John Anthony West, *Gladys's Gregory*

A Note to Chocoholics

Unsweetened cocoa powder is a form of chocolate with some of the cocoa butter removed. Not, alas, all the cocoa butter; cocoa powder is not fat-free. At about 22% fat, for most cocoa powders it is a slightly lower-fat form of chocolate. Some people (I am one) consider chocolate one of life's essentials. It has a dark, erotic quality that speaks to the emotions as well as the tastebuds. It is possible, I am delighted to say, to obtain a truly low-fat cocoa powder (12%). Although the fat has been drastically reduced, there is no loss of taste or quality. See the Mail Order Guide (page 161) for information. You will find my Slim Cuisine chocolate creations intensely chocolaty; they are therapeutic but not for bingeing. Eat them occasionally, but don't overdo it.

MILK CHOCOLATE JELLY

Makes 25 fl oz/750 ml

Both the chocolate jelly and following orange jelly can be un-moulded on to a Meringue Pie Shell (page 146) and surrounded by satsuma or mandarin sections, strawberries and raspberries; or they can be chilled in a bowl until set and then spooned into small meringue shells. If spooning into small meringue shells, use only 1 sachet gelatine in the recipe. Try orange jelly in chocolate meringue, and chocolate jelly in white meringue. One more suggestion: if you unmould the jelly on to a Meringue Pie Shell, try surrounding it with *frozen* raspberries and cherries. As they thaw, their juices are released and the meringue turns gooey (the chocolate meringue becomes fudgy). It's quite impossibly delicious and satisfying on a very basic level.

2 sachets gelatine	*12 fl oz/360 ml skimmed milk*
12 fl oz/360 ml hot water	*3 tablespoons fat-reduced cocoa*
8 tablespoons caster sugar	*(see page 155), sifted*
½ teaspoon vanilla essence	*6–7 tablespoons fromage frais*

1   Mix the gelatine into the hot water. Stir until thoroughly dissolved. Stir in sugar and let it dissolve. Stir in vanilla, milk and cocoa. Chill until the mixture is thickened and almost completely set.
2   Scrape into a cold bowl and whip with an electric mixer until fluffy and very smooth. Thoroughly beat in the fromage frais. Everything must be very well amalgamated. Pour into a mould and chill overnight until totally set. Unmould and serve.

ORANGE CREAM JELLY

Makes 25 fl oz/750 ml

For Easter, chill the orange jelly and chocolate jelly in bunny moulds, and unmould on to meringue nests.

25 fl oz/750 ml strained, freshly	*2–3 tablespoons caster sugar*
squeezed orange juice	*6–7 tablespoons fromage frais*
2 sachets gelatine	

1   Pour 4 fl oz/120 ml orange juice into a saucepan. Sprinkle in the gelatine. Stir over low heat until warm and dissolved. Do not let it come to a simmer. Stir in sugar and let dissolve.

2   Pour in the remaining juice. Chill until thickened and almost set.
3   Scrape into a cold bowl and whip until fluffy and perfectly smooth with an electric beater. Thoroughly beat in the fromage frais. Everything must be well amalgamated. Pour into a mould and chill overnight. Unmould and serve.

ORANGES WITH ORANGE BRANDY

I like to make this beautiful dessert with a combination of blood oranges and ordinary ones. What a radiant and refreshing way to end a meal!

Oranges, 2 per person	*Candied Peel (optional, see below)*
Orange liqueur (Cointreau or	*Fromage frais*
Grand Marnier)	*Brown sugar*

1   Peel the oranges over a bowl to catch the juices. Peel so that the zest and the bitter pith come away. (If you are making the Candied Peel, use a zester to remove the zest. Cut away the pith with a knife, and discard.)
2   On a cutting board, slice the oranges about ¼ inch/0.6 cm thick.
3   Overlap the slices on pretty glass plates (two oranges per plate). Pour the juices from the bowl and the cutting board evenly over the slices. Pour ½ tablespoon of orange liqueur over each plate of slices and scatter on a bit of peel.
4   Set aside until needed. Centre a dollop of fromage frais on each arrangement of slices, and sprinkle each dollop with ¼ teaspoon brown sugar. Serve at once.

Candied Peel

Julienned zest of 2–4 oranges	*2 fl oz/60 ml water*
2 fl oz/60 ml orange liqueur	
(Cointreau or Grand Marnier)	

1   Combine zest, orange liqueur and water in a small non-reactive frying pan. Bring to a slow simmer.
2   Simmer very slowly, stirring occasionally, until all the liquid is evaporated. Spread out on greaseproof paper to cool. Refrigerate until needed.

♡ Omit peel.

Slim Cuisine Ice Cream

As an American, I was born with an ice cream gene, the way the English are born with a tea gene, and the French with a champagne gene. In America, the butterfat level of ice cream is sky high, and every supermarket has endless aisles of freezer cases, overflowing with 'designer' ice creams: elegant packaging, enough butterfat to choke a brontosaurus and vividly intense flavours. To make things even more outrageous, many of the supermarkets (foodie seduction markets, really) are open 24 hours a day, *every day in the year*. When one is overcome by an ice cream attack, even at 3 a.m., it can be satisfied in minutes. A pint of macadamia nut-chocolate chip, two spoons and thou beside me in the bed . . . Paradise indeed. When I moved to England almost five years ago, the 24-hour seduction markets with their compelling freezer cabinets were far away. And I had foresworn butterfat anyway. What to do about those cravings? My solution to the ice cream dilemma has reached the status of legend. The Slim Cuisine ice cream recipes from *Slim Cuisine I* get fan letters. For instance: 'The banana ice cream is terrific! Couldn't believe how rich and creamy it was', or 'I have honestly never tasted any ice cream more delicious', and 'Every time that I make your ice cream, I thank you out loud and so do my family and friends. It's unbelievable!!!! and you are a heroine.' Under the circumstances, I thought it best to repeat the ice cream technique here. It is an instant technique, so if *you* get an ice cream attack at 3 a.m., pull out the frozen fruit, dump it in the food processor, pour in the buttermilk and presto!, the best cold comfort in the world.

♡ ⊕ ⑤ BANANA ICE CREAM

Makes approximately 1¾ pts/840 ml

---

4 bananas, peeled, cut into chunks, and frozen (they should be frozen so that you have separate pieces, not a large frozen mass)	*½ teaspoon vanilla essence* *3–4 tablespoons* *NutraSweet/Canderel* *5 fl oz/150 ml buttermilk*

---

1   Place the frozen banana chunks in the container of the food processor. Add the vanilla, sweetener and half the buttermilk.
2   Turn on the processor and let it run for a few moments. Then, while it is running, pour in the remaining buttermilk in a thin, steady stream. Let the machine run until the mixture is beautifully smooth and creamy. Spoon into bowls and serve at once.

'I doubt whether the world holds for anyone a more soul-stirring surprise than the first adventure with ice cream.'

Heywood Broun, *Seeing Things at Night*

♡ ⊕ ⑤ RASPBERRY ICE CREAM
Makes approximately 1¼ pts/840 ml

12 oz/360 g packet frozen raspberries (unsweetened)	4–5 tablespoons NutraSweet/Canderel
6–8 fl oz/180–240 ml cold buttermilk	

1 Do not thaw the berries. Dump them, still frozen, into the bowl of a food processor or liquidizer. Pour in half of the buttermilk and sprinkle in the sweetener.
2 Turn on the machine. Process for a few seconds, stopping to scrape down the sides if necessary.
3 With the machine running, pour in the remaining buttermilk. Process until the mixture forms a super-creamy ice cream. Spoon into clear glass goblets and serve at once.

Note: Of course you can use this instant ice cream technique with any frozen fruit you choose, as long as you have *separate* frozen pieces, not a large mass. Try peaches, strawberries, blueberries, pitted cherries, mango, etc.

♡ ▨ ⊕ CAPPUCINO
Cappucino – strong coffee topped with frothy steamed milk – is usually made with full-fat milk or half cream. Even if you have no cappucino machine to steam the milk and you don't touch whole milk or cream, you can still make a beautifully frothy, creamy mug of cappucino at home. You need good coffee, a microwave, a liquidizer and skimmed milk.

Skimmed milk	Fat-reduced cocoa powder (see page 155)
Filtered coffee, made from dark roasted coffee beans	

1 Bring the milk just to the boil. (The microwave is perfect for this.) Pour some of the milk into the liquidizer container. (Fill it a little less than half, or you may splash and burn yourself, and make a terrible mess.) Turn the machine on; wait a moment, then carefully lift up a tiny corner of the lid on the side away

from you so that some air gets in. *Be careful* – stand back and avert your face slightly. Blend on high for 50–60 seconds. Pour the milk into a jug. Repeat until all milk has been whipped.

2   Fill coffee cup or mugs ½–⅔ full. Top up with milk, including some of the froth. With a tea strainer, sift a tiny bit of cocoa on to each mugful. Serve at once.

CELEBRATION PUNCH

Makes 11 pts/6600 ml/55 punch cup servings

I devised this party drink when the 'Daytime Live' folks asked me to develop a festive non-alcoholic drink for the last show of the season.

---

3 pts/1800 ml strong lemon verbena tea
2½ pts/1500 ml cranberry juice
2½/900 ml low-Calorie American dry ginger ale

1½ pts/900 ml low-Calorie sparkling lemonade
Strawberry ice cubes (see below)

Combine all ingredients, except ice cubes. Serve the punch ice-cold. Add the strawberry ice cubes at the last minute.

Note: This recipe can be scaled down if desired.

Strawberry Ice Cubes
Quarter fresh strawberries. Put a quarter berry in each compartment of ice cube trays. Fill with water and freeze.

🕐   Omit strawberry ice cubes.

🕐   ALCOHOL-FREE SANGRIA

Makes 7 pts/4200 ml

Just the thing for picnics and barbecues. It tastes quite alcoholic. You may find that people become slightly tipsy through the power of suggestion, if you don't tell them how innocent the drink is.

---

16 fl oz/500 ml chilled fresh orange juice
1 box (36 fl oz/1 litre chilled cranberry juice

2 limes
1 pt/600 ml sparkling mineral water

---

1   In a jug, stir together the orange and cranberry juices. Halve the limes, and squeeze in their juice. Drop the squeezed lime halves into the jug. Refrigerate.

2   Pour in the water just before serving.

Mail Order Guide

Write or telephone for a price
   list.

Anton's Delicatessen 101 Hare Lane Claygate Esher Surrey KT10 0QX Tel: 0372 62306	Tinned tortillas Mexican specialities Balsamic vinegar Dry pack sun-dried tomatoes
Books for Cooks 4 Blenheim Crescent London W11 1NN Tel: 01 221 1992	Dry pack sun-dried tomatoes
Culpeper Limited Hadstock Road Linton Cambridgeshire CB1 6NJ Tel: 0223 894054	Californian dry pack sun-dried tomatoes, no added salt
Italian Taste 32 Abbeygate Street Bury St Edmunds Suffolk Tel: 0284 752605	Dry pack sun-dried tomatoes Balsamic vinegar Quick-cooking polenta Dried mushrooms

Health Craze
Cromwell Court
115 Earls Court Road
London
SW5
Tel: 01 244 7784

Parsons Trading Ltd
Orion House
Gray's Place
Slough
Berkshire
SL2 5AF
Tel: 0753 26196

Vegetable stock powders and
  pastes including Friggs
  Vegetale and Healthrite stock
  paste
Pulses and dried beans,
  including black beans

Excellent quality fat-reduced
  cocoa powder

Index

163

mushy peas, Montezuma's 44–45
mustard, New York deli 138
mustard sauce with pork 72–73

nachos 42–43
nachos, potato skin 43
New Orleans style gratin of red
  beans 95–96
New York breakfast 35
New York deli mustard 138

onion(s)
  caramelized, and bread soufflé
    105–106
  fried 23
  herbed for polenta 117–118
  herbed with grilled polenta 116
  sautéed spring 125–126
  spring, gratin of 126
  tears 19
orange cream jelly 156–157
oranges with orange brandy 33,
  36, 157
Oriental chicken salad 94

pan-'fried' mushrooms 22, 34
pan-'fried' potatoes 34, 130–131
Parmesan cheese 26
pasta with creamy fennel sauce
  100–101
pastry, filo (phyllo) 39–41, 150
pastry, strudel 39–41
pâté, chicken liver 36, 41
patties, sausage 34, 36, 84–85
peas, Montezuma's mushy 44–45
peel, candied 157
pepper(s)
  marinated 136–137
  red, and garlic spread 45
  red, and tomato borscht 48–49
  salad 113
  savoury 124
  stir 'fried' 25
  stuffed 80–81
  to grill 24
  to microwave 24
  to peel 24
  vegetable stuffed 123–124
  with cauliflower 36, 122–123
pepper-potato stew 111–112
pepper-tomato sauce 80
peppered steak with mushroom
  sauce 65–66
pesto 17
pesto chicken potato salad 33, 93
phyllo pastry 39–41, 150
picnics 32–33
pie, curried shepherd's 77–78
pie, mince 36, 150
pie, shepherd's 75–76
pilaf, wheat 134
piperade potatoes 109–110
piquant chicken 90–91
pizzas, tortilla 43
plum jam 34, 140
poached pears in honeyed red
  wine 142
polenta, general information 114
polenta, grilled with herbed
  onions, or intense mushroom
  ragoût 116
polenta, layered with aubergine
  114–115
popcorn 7
porcini mushrooms 27
pork
  in mustard sauce 72–73

sausage patties 34, 36, 84–85
tenderloin 72–73
potato(s)
  chicken pesto salad 33, 93
  chilli 112–113 ▲
  'fried' 131
  mashed 108
  mashed, general information
    107
  nachos, potato skin 43
  pan-'fried' 34, 130–131
  pepper stew 111–112
  piperade 109–110
  ragoût, Hungarian 110–111
  roast 31, 36, 132
  salad, spicy 33, 135–136
  stefado 111
  turnip ratatouille 113–114
  veal balls 81–82
poultry
  chicken liver kebabs 86–87
  chicken with mango sauce 92
  chicken pesto potato salad 93
  lemon roasted chicken 92–93
  Oriental chicken salad 94
  piquant chicken 90–91
  roast chicken 89–90
  roast turkey 87–88
  tandoori chicken 91
prawn sauce with asparagus
  61–62
prunes in lemon sauce 140
pudding, bread 31, 147–148
pudding, bread with mincemeat
  36, 149–150
pudding, chocolate bread 148–149
pudding, semolina – cold version
  153
pudding, semolina – warm
  version 154
punch, celebration 160
purée, aubergine 21
purée, garlic 17
purée, raspberry with strawberries
  36, 129–130
purée of swede, turnip and white
  bean 36, 129–130

quark 25
quick breakfasts 34

ragoût
  Hungarian potato 110–111
  intense mushroom 118
  tomato-broad bean 117
  tomato-broad bean with grilled
    polenta 116
raspberry ice cream 159
raspberry sauce with strawberries
  33, 141
ratatouille, turnip-potato 113–114
raw vegetables 4, 6
reconstituted dried mushrooms
  119
red bean gratin, New Orleans
  style 95–96
red pepper and garlic spread 45
red pepper and tomato borscht
  48–49
rillettes, lamb 39
roast chicken 89–90
roast lamb 31, 73–74
roast potatoes 31, 36, 132
roast turkey 36, 87–88
roasted lemon chicken 92–93
root vegetable soup 52–53
rump skirt steak 66, 69–72

Russian dressing 62
rutabagas 128

salad(s)
  chicken pesto potato 33, 93
  mango and tomato 135
  Oriental chicken 94
  pepper 113
  spicy potato 33, 135–136
samosa, lamb 39–41
samosa, lamb filling for 40
samosa, vegetable 41
sandwiches 46
sangria, alcohol-free 160
sauce(s)
  aubergine-sausage for pasta 85
  chocolate cream 154–155
  creamy fennel, with pasta
    100–101
  creamy herb dressing 137
  lemon cream 36, 151
  lemon with prunes 140
  mango with chicken 92
  mushroom with peppered steak
    65–66
  mustard with pork 72–73
  pesto 17
  prawn with asparagus 61–62
  sausage-aubergine for pasta 85
  soy 27
  spicy bean for pasta 98–99
  teriyaki 27
  tomato 16
  tomato-pepper 80
  yoghurt herb 81
sausage mix, for stuffing 89
sausage patties 34, 36, 84–85
sausage-aubergine sauce for pasta
  85
sautéed mushrooms 22
sautéed spring onions 125–126
sautéing in stock 10
savoury peppers 124
semolina pudding – cold version
  153
semolina pudding – warm version
  154
shallots, braised 125
shepherd's pie 75–76
shepherd's pie, curried 77–78
shiitake mushrooms 27
side dishes
  baked courgettes, Italian style
    127–128
  braised carrots 124–125
  braised leeks 127
  braised shallots 125
  cauliflower and peppers
    122–123
  'fried' potatoes 131
  green bean soufflé 122
  kasha with mushrooms 132–134
  marinated carrots 137
  marinated peppers 136–137
  pan-'fried' potatoes with onions
    130–131
  purée of swede, turnip and
    white beans 129–130
  roast potatoes 132
  sautéed spring onions 125–126
  savoury peppers 124
  spicy sprouts 128
  vegetable stuffed peppers
    123–124
  wheat pilaf 134
  whipped swedes 128–129
skirt steak, goose 63–67

165

skirt steak, rump 66, 69–72
Slim Cuisine ice cream 158
Slim Cuisine mincemeat 150
Slim Cuisine regime 3–5
smoky fish chowder 59
snacks 5–8
sole with vermouth 60
soufflé(s)
  banana 144
  bread and caramelized onion
    105–106
  of caramelized bananas 152–153
  chocolate 145
  general information 143
  green bean 122
  mango 144–145
soup(s)
  black bean 53–54
  California-style cioppino 58–59
  fish 54–55
  goulash 51
  lettuce and fennel 48
  root vegetable 52–53
  smoky fish chowder 59
  vegetable 50
soy sauce 27
spicy bean sauce for pasta 98–99
spicy Brussels sprouts 36, 128
spread, chive 46
spread, garlic 46
spreads, for sandwiches 46
spring onion gratin, 126
spring onions, sautéed 125–126
starters, spreads and snacks
  artichoke toasts 44
  chicken liver pâté 41–42
  chive spread 46
  lamb samosa 39–41
  mock guacamole 44–45
  nachos 42–43
  red pepper and garlic spread 45
  slim sandwiches 46
  vegetable canapés 38–39
steak, goose skirt, grilled 33, 67
steak, peppered with mushroom
  sauce 65–66
steamed fish bundle 60–61
stefado of beef 71–72
stefado, potato 111
stew, potato-pepper 111–112
stir 'fried' peppers 25
stock
  chicken 13
  desperation 15
  fish 14
  powdered 10–11
  sautéing with 10

strawberry ice cubes 160
strawberries, with raspberry sauce
  33, 141
strudel pastry 39–41
stufatino 70–71
stuffed cabbage, sweet and sour
  78–80
stuffed mushrooms 33, 35
stuffed peppers 80–81
stuffing, chestnut 36, 88–89
sun-dried tomatoes 27
Sunday lunch 30
swede, turnip and white bean,
  purée of 36, 129–130
swedes, whipped 31, 128–129
sweet and sour stuffed cabbage
  78–80
sweet bar substitute 7
symbols, explained 11

Tamale pie meatballs, Marjorie
  Hoek's 83–84
tandoori chicken 91
tenderloin, pork 72–73
teriyaki sauce 27
therapeutic binge 11
tinned vegetables 28
toast, French 147
tomatoes
  broad bean ragoût 117
  broad bean ragoût with grilled
    polenta 116
  grilled 34
  and mango salad 135
  pepper sauce 80
  sauce 16
  sun-dried 27
torte, fudgy chocolate 145–146
tortilla chips 7, 98
tortilla pizzas 43
tortillas 98
tortillas, baked 43
turkey, roast 36, 87–88
turnip, white bean and swede,
  purée of 36, 129–130
turnip-potato ratatouille 113–114

veal sausage mix 89
veal shanks with wild mushrooms
  74–75
veal-potato balls 81–82
vegetable canapés 33, 36, 38
vegetable(s)
  curry for couscous 101–102
  frozen 28
  gumbo 119–120
  platter 126

raw 4, 6
root soup 52–53
samosa 41
soup 50
stuffed peppers 123–124
tinned 28
vegetarian main dishes
  black bean chilaquiles 97
  black beans 96
  bread and caramelized onion
    soufflé 105–106
  chilaquiles 99–100
  chilli 103–104
  couscous with vegetables
    101–102
  gratin of red beans New
    Orleans style 95–96
  grilled polenta with herbed
    onions or intense mushroom
    ragoût 116
  grilled polenta with tomato-
    broad bean ragoût 116
  Hungarian potato ragoût
    110–111
  intense mushroom ragoût 116, 118
  lasagne 104–105
  layered polenta and aubergine
    114–115
  mashed potatoes 108
  pasta with creamy fennel sauce
    100–101
  piperade potatoes 109–110
  potato chilli 112–113
  potato stefado 111
  potato-pepper stew 111–112
  spicy bean sauce for pasta
    98–99
  tomato-broad bean ragoût 117
  turnip-potato ratatouille
    113–114
  vegetable gumbo 119–120
vinegar, balsamic 26
vitamin D 32
vitamins, fat-soluble 4, 32

wheat pilaf 134
whipped swede 31, 128–129
white bean, swede and turnip,
  purée of 36, 129–130
wild mushrooms with veal shanks
  74–75

yoghurt-herb fillings 39
yoghurt herb sauce 81
yolks, egg 3–4

zester 50